JOHN FARLAM was born in Stockport, Ches driver training industry in 1979. As an expe training courses his contributions to driving and the innovative *SmartDriving Instructor'* ideas to driver training in the UK. He is curre *Driving Magazine* and *The Driving Instructo*

GW00360754

He opened his first driving school in south London in the early 1980s before moving to west Sussex. His skills later took him to Yorkshire where he was training director for a national driving school. His extensive experience has included the development and teaching of advanced driving, skid prevention, risk avoidance and 'anti road-rage' courses. In addition, he has trained many trainers of driving instructors and, in his role as instructor consultant, he has helped hundreds of driving instructors to improve their day-to-day teaching skills. His qualifications include UK Approved Driving Instructor, DIR (Ireland) Registered Driving Instructor, RAC Registered Driving Instructor, Diamond Advanced Driving Instructor, ROSPA Advanced Teaching Diploma and classroom teaching certificates. He has also used his psychotherapeutic and counselling skills to help road traffic accident victims who have been traumatised by their experiences.

Based in Ireland, John now concentrates his efforts on the further development of driving skills through his road safety website – www.smartdriving.co.uk – and regular training visits to the UK.

YOU'VE PASSED!

A Complete Guide to the Driving Test

JOHN FARLAM

THE
BLACKSTAFF
PRESS

BELFAST

ACKNOWLEDGEMENTS

My thanks go to Gabriel Barry of the Department of the
Environment and Local Government for his help with details
about the driving test, and to my wife Phyl for her endless
patience during the writing of this book.

J.F.

First published in 1998 by
Blackstaff Press Limited
Wildflower Way, Apollo Road, Belfast BT12 6TA, Northern Ireland

Reprinted 2002

John Farlam has asserted his right under the
Copyright, Designs and Patents Act 1988 to be identified as
the author of this work.

Designed and laid out using CorelDraw computer softwear

Printed in England by Biddles Limited

A CIP catalogue record for this book
is available from the British Library

ISBN 0-85640-623-6

Contents

Section Three: Applying your skills

Section Four: The driving test

Section Five: After you've passed!

Introduction

Driver's Notes:

# Introduction

Congratulations on choosing *You've Passed* to prepare for your driving test. *You've Passed* is designed to help you to develop all the skills needed for everyday driving, ranging from slow-speed manoeuvres to high-speed motorway cruising. It doesn't matter if you've never driven before or if you have already had some driving experience, the *You've Passed* method can help you make quick and easy progress towards your driving test and lay the foundations for a lifetime of safe driving.

Five easy sections

- **Section One** helps you to build all the basic skills needed to control the car safely.

- **Section Two** provides you with a sound knowledge of how to approach hazards.

- **Section Three** shows you how to apply your newly acquired skills and knowledge in a wide range of everyday situations.

- **Section Four** gives information about preparing for and taking the driving test.

- **Section Five** offers help and advice about your safety after you have passed your test and includes subjects ranging from motorways to road rage.

Structured training

You've Passed is structured so that you learn new skills in a logical, progressive order. As you work through the book, each new skill is introduced when you are ready for it and builds naturally on what you have already learned. This will make your learning easy and enjoyable.

By using *You've Passed* in conjunction with your practical training, you will get maximum value from every minute that you spend behind the wheel.

To gain the full benefit from *You've Passed* you should work through the first two sections in the order that they are presented in the book. Your instructor will help you to decide the best order for the subjects covered later in the book.

Lessons and quizzes

As you read through the book you will find a series of *Practical Lessons*, *Quizzes* and useful information.

The best and quickest way to learn is by doing your training in small, easy steps. In order to achieve this, ask your instructor what you will be covering next then read the relevant *Practical Lesson* information and answer the quiz questions.

The quizzes in this book are designed so that you can mark them yourself. You won't find a list of answers in the book; all the answers can be found either on the page before the quiz or in *The Highway Code*.

By searching for the answers you will reinforce your learning and accelerate your progress. If you prefer, you can cheat! Look for the answers first. Because of the easy-to-follow way that *You've Passed* is designed, you will still learn quickly and easily.

Getting the most from your time in the car

You are already finding out how *You've Passed* has been developed to help you to learn more quickly and to save you money on your practical lessons.

By reading about your lesson and completing the quiz questions before you go out in the car, you will gain more benefit from your practice. Reading the same material after you drive will help you to remember and to better understand your positive experiences in the car.

Sometimes, a lesson in your car will include topics from more than one of the *Practical Lessons* in this book. You might take two or three lessons in the car to cover one *Practical Lesson* from the book. There is no fixed rule, every driver is different! As you work through

the book you will sign off each lesson when you become competent.

Signing off is done at two levels:

1 When you cover a new subject for the first time and do it with lots of help you will sign your book and record the date of the lesson.

2 When you can perform the same skill unassisted you will sign and date the relevant page to show that you are one step nearer the goal of passing your test.

By signing off your lessons you will ensure that you always have a clear and objective view of where you are in the course and how long it is likely to be before you are ready for your driving test.

How many driving lessons will I need before my test?

You will find lots of people willing to offer advice on this subject. Well-meaning advice and guidance can often mislead. Advice such as, 'You only need a few lessons to learn the test route' or 'I passed after 10 lessons – nobody needs more than that' can often leave learners feeling inadequate. People learn in different circumstances and at different rates; you are an individual and will learn at your own pace.

There is no reliable formula for working out how long it will take to learn to drive; the number of lessons needed varies from person to person. As a general rule, the older you are the longer it takes to learn. However, there are plenty of examples to prove this rule wrong.

No matter what age you are, you should expect to take at least 25 hours' training with a driving instructor.

There's an old saying: 'Safe driving is no accident.' Remember, it's not learning quickly that makes a good driver, it's learning correctly.

Choosing your driving instructor

Some people learn to drive with friends and relatives, but as roads get busier it's wise for all learners to have some lessons with a professional instructor. Make sure that your instructor is a qualified ADI (Driving Standards Agency Approved Driving Instructor). It is illegal for anyone who is not an ADI to charge a fee for driving tuition.

Your instructor will guide you carefully through your training and ensure that you are fully prepared to drive safely after passing your test. Another valuable reason for taking lessons with

an ADI is that you might be able to save money on your motor insurance after taking a post-test Pass Plus course.

Practising with friends and family

If you have an opportunity to practise driving between lessons you should take it. The more driving practice you can get, the quicker you will learn and pass your test.

Although you will learn quicker if you get more practice, I do have a word of warning. When practising with friends or relatives, remember that they are the ones with the experience. Listen to their advice and act upon it. If the advice given by friends is different from that of your instructor, find out why. Get your friends to talk to your instructor about the most modern and efficient driving techniques.

Down to business

Now you know what to do, it's time to make a start. Remember, take it step by step and it will be easy.

Good Luck !!

Driver's Notes:

Section One

Basic Forward
Driving Skills

Driver's Notes:

Before you start learning to drive

There are some important points that you must be aware of before you start to drive. The first, and perhaps most important of all, is that as a driver you are legally responsible for your vehicle, your own safety and the safety of all those around you. This applies from the very first time you sit behind the wheel even though you are only a learner.

Eligibility to drive

- You must be at least 17 years of age (unless registered disabled).

- You must hold a valid provisional licence for the vehicle that you are learning to drive in.

- You must comply with the conditions of your driving licence.

- You must be accompanied by someone over 21 years of age who has held a full driving licence for a minimum of three years.

- You must be properly insured to drive. If in doubt, check with your insurance company.

Your vehicle

- must be legally roadworthy

- must display a valid road tax disc

- must display clearly visible **L** plates to the front and rear. (Note that cars displaying **L** plates in Northern Ireland are restricted to 45 mph.)

Seatbelts and safety

Seatbelts are provided in modern cars to help ensure the safety of the driver and passengers. Seatbelts cannot guarantee your safety – only safe driving can do that. However, they will greatly reduce your risk of serious injury.

You must

- check the anchorages and fittings of your seatbelts and ensure that they are free from all obvious defects;

- wear a seatbelt when driving (unless you have been granted exemption);

- ensure that any passengers aged 14 years and under comply with the requirements to wear a seatbelt or suitable restraint.

Alcohol and the driver

Attempting to drive after drinking alcohol can lead to a lifetime of guilt and misery if you kill another innocent road user. There is no nice way to explain this message. Some people will try to tell you that one or two drinks won't do any harm. Don't listen; drinking and driving can wreck your life and the lives of others.

The only guaranteed safe level of alcohol when driving is none at all. Don't celebrate passing your driving test by losing your licence. **Drinking and driving wrecks lives …**

? Driving quiz
Before you start learning to drive

1 When visiting a friend who has a driving test later in the day, you find that he/she is very nervous. Would you advise your friend to (tick one answer):

○ take a few deep breaths and try to relax?

○ go for a 10-minute drive alone to boost his/her confidence?

○ have a drink to calm the nerves?

2 Who is responsible for ensuring that a 13-year-old boy wears his seatbelt in a car that you are driving (tick one answer)?

○ no one – it's up to him

○ you, the driver

○ the boy's parents

3 Complete the following sentence:

As a driver, I am legally responsible for ensuring that any car I drive is legally r................. , is displaying a r........... t........... disc and is properly i................... for me to drive.

Progress check ✓

I know and understand my basic responsibilities as a driver.

○ Signed .... Date ....

I am fully aware of the restrictions that are placed on the holders of provisional driving licences.

○ Signed .... Date ....

Cockpit drill
Practical lesson

The cockpit drill is a routine that you will carry out each time you get into the driving seat. The drill is necessary to ensure that you can reach all the controls and that you have a clear view from the vehicle.

The items that you check in your cockpit drill are:

Doors

Make sure that all the car doors, including hatchbacks, are closed properly. This also entails using child locks if you are carrying young children.

Seat

Can you reach the pedals? You should be able to press the pedal on the left (the clutch pedal) down to the floor with your left foot without stretching your leg.

Steering

The backrest of your seat and steering height (if applicable) should be adjusted so that you can reach the steering wheel comfortably. Make sure that the head restraint is positioned with the middle part level with your ears.

Seatbelts

All car occupants must wear seatbelts, if they are fitted. As the driver, you are legally responsible for ensuring that seatbelts are worn by children aged 14 and under.

ALL OCCUPANTS!

Mirrors

You must ensure that your mirrors are correctly positioned before you start to drive. Adjust the mirrors to give the best possible view behind with minimal head movement when sitting in your normal driving position.

Remember: DSSSM

? Driving quiz
Cockpit drill

1 Complete the following words to list the items in the cockpit drill:

D .... **S** .... **S** .... **S** .... **M** ....

2 When checking your seat adjustment, you press down the clutch pedal.
   If the seat is correctly adjusted your left leg should be (tick one answer):

   ☐ stretched out
   ☐ slightly bent

3 Head restraints should be adjusted so that the middle part
   is level with (tick one answer):

   ☐ the base of your neck
   ☐ the top of your head
   ☐ your ears

4 In some cars you may have to adjust the outside mirrors before you
   put on your seatbelt.

   TRUE ◯

   FALSE ◯

Progress check ✓

I can complete my cockpit drill:

with help from my instructor   ◯ Signed .... Date ....

without help from my instructor   ◯ Signed .... Date ....

Foot controls
Training notes

Accelerator pedal

The accelerator is operated by your right foot and controls the power from the engine. When you press the accelerator the engine produces more power to make the car go faster; releasing the pedal reduces the power and will usually slow the car down (unless you are going downhill).

Your instructor may use the term 'gas pedal' when referring to the accelerator. This is done for ease of instruction and understanding – 'more gas', for example, would mean press the pedal a bit harder, 'less gas', a little less.

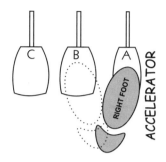

Footbrake pedal

Like the accelerator, you operate the footbrake with your right foot. This pedal operates brakes on all the wheels to slow, or stop, the car. The footbrake also switches on the brake lights at the back of the car so that drivers behind you know that you are slowing down.

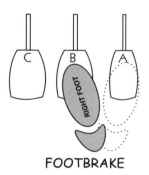

Clutch pedal

The clutch pedal is operated with your left foot. When the pedal is pressed down the link between the engine and the driving wheels is broken; this allows you to change gear and stop the car without stopping the engine.

As soon as you have learned the basic skill of moving off and stopping you will learn about 'clutch control'. This is a way of using the clutch pedal to make the car move very slowly and is an essential skill in many driving situations.

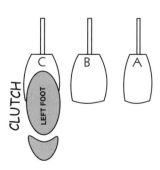

❓ Driving quiz
Foot controls

1 Your instructor may use an alternative name for the accelerator; is this (tick one answer):

☐ the gas pedal?
☐ the power pedal?
☐ the speed pedal?

2 When you press the footbrake pedal the car will slow down. What else does the footbrake pedal do?

3 The diagrams below show a simple representation of the clutch. Mark each diagram to show whether you think the clutch pedal is up or down (based upon the information about the clutch on the previous page).

The clutch pedal is

ENGINE

ENGINE

The clutch pedal is

Progress check ✓

I can locate and explain the purpose and use of the foot controls:

with help from my instructor   ◯ Signed .... Date ....

without help from my instructor   ◯ Signed .... Date ....

Hand controls
Practical lesson

Steering wheel

The steering wheel turns the car to the left or right. One of the best ways to remember where to position your hands on the wheel is to imagine a clock face. Your hands should be horizontally opposite, with your left hand between 9 and 10 and your right hand between 2 and 3. Holding the steering wheel like this will usually give you maximum control over the car, especially in an emergency situation.

Indicator switch

This switch is usually mounted behind the steering wheel and 'fingertip-operated'; it activates the flashing indicators to the front, rear and sides of the car. By using the indicators **before** you change direction, you can show other road users which way you intend to go (signals are covered in detail on pages 41–2).

Gear lever

Most cars have four or five forward gears and one reverse gear. The gears are used to drive at different speeds and can be selected by pressing the clutch pedal down and then moving the gear lever to the appropriate position (changing gear is covered in detail on pages 25–6). Thinking of the gear layout for the first four gears as an **H** shape will help you to remember where they are. The position of reverse gear varies from car to car.

Handbrake

The handbrake is used to secure the car after it has stopped. It might help to think of it as a parking brake. You must never use the handbrake when the car is moving.

? Driving quiz
Hand controls

1 Mark the steering wheel below to show where you would place your hands for maximum control.

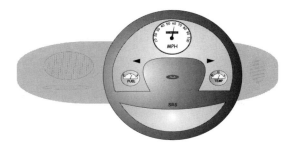

2 You should never use the handbrake when the car is moving.

TRUE ◯   FALSE ◯

3 The indicator switch is mounted behind the steering wheel; it should be operated by (tick one answer):

☐ the palm of your hand

☐ a tight grip

☐ your fingertips

Progress check ✓

I can explain the purpose of the hand controls.   ◯ Signed .... Date ....

I can use the hand controls with help and/or prompting from my instructor.   ◯ Signed .... Date ....

I can use the hand controls without any assistance.   ◯ Signed .... Date ....

Light switches
Training notes

So many switches!

Your instructor will not cover all the controls when first introducing you to the car. The reasons for this are:

1 you would have too much to remember;
2 you could easily become bored with so much theory;
3 the sooner you can start driving the car the better.

The following controls will be introduced as and when they are needed.

Light switches

Light switches are in different places in different cars. However, they all usually have two positions. The first position switches on the side lights (parking lights). In modern cars the side lights brighten up as soon as the ignition is switched on; this setting, dim–dip, is automatic. Dim–dip lights are considered to be safer than side lights when driving in built-up areas at night because it makes cars easier to see. The second position switches on the headlights (these can be dipped or full-beam).

In addition to the main light switch there is a 'dip' switch. This switch is often mounted behind the steering wheel and may be incorporated into the indicator switch. The dip switch allows you to easily change from dipped beam (a short beam that won't dazzle other drivers) to full beam (a long beam for use on clear, open roads).

Other light switches might include front and rear fog lights and spot lights. Front fog lights are primarily for use when driving at night in the fog. They are designed so that the light is not reflected back to the driver (by the moisture droplets in the air) so giving you better vision. You must switch off your headlights when using front fog lights at night in order to gain maximum benefit.

Rear fog lights are high-intensity red lights for use in very poor visibility. Think of your rear fog lights as signals to let other drivers know that you are there. As soon as there is a car close behind, switch them off. You should take great care in the use of these lights as they can dazzle drivers behind you and mask the effect of your brake lights.

Main light
switch

Parking lights

Dipped
headlights

Full-beam
headlights

Front
fog lights

Rear
fog lights

Other controls

Horn

The horn is often situated on the same stalk switch as the indicators, but some cars have the horn switch placed in the centre of the steering wheel. You should only use the horn to warn other drivers of your presence. Avoid using the horn when your car is stationary, or at night in a built-up area.

Heater

Most cars are fitted with a heater to keep passengers warm and comfortable. The heater usually has three switches: these control the temperature setting, the 'blower' (fan) speed and the direction of the airflow. By varying the settings of these switches you can control the temperature inside the car.

De-misters

In cold or wet weather the car windows often get misted up. To help avoid this problem your car has a de-mister system. The windscreen de-mister is often an integral part of the heating system. The rear de-mister is usually a series of heated wires that are embedded in the glass of the screen. Although many rear de-misters switch off automatically after a set time period, you should always check to ensure that they are not left on unnecessarily; the high power consumption could drain your car battery.

FRONT

REAR

Windscreen wipers

The front wipers (and washers) are often operated by a fingertip stalk switch behind the steering wheel. Most modern cars have a two-speed setting and an intermittent setting. Rear wipers are sometimes operated by the same switch as the front wipers. However, some cars have a separate switch on the dashboard.

FRONT

REAR

Choke

When a petrol engine is cold, it needs a different mixture of fuel and air to run efficiently. The choke control adjusts this mixture. The choke gets its name because it 'chokes' off some of the air supply to the engine, thus making the petrol mixture stronger.

Hazard warning lights

The switch for the hazard warning lights turns on all the indicators simultaneously; it is usually large and orange. Hazard warning lights are not an excuse for bad parking; they should only be used if your vehicle becomes an obstruction and/or danger on the road.

Rear view mirrors
Practical lesson

Why you need mirrors

When you are driving, you need to know what is happening all around you, all the time. Before making a decision to change your speed or position you must know exactly where the traffic behind you is and how fast it's travelling. This information is essential for safety. If when you check your mirrors you find that there is a problem behind, you may need to change your plans. This forms the basis of the **Mirrors – Signal – Manoeuvre** routine.

Two types of mirror

There are two types of mirror fitted to motor cars – flat and convex. In most cars (but not all) the interior mirror is flat and the door mirrors are convex.

When you see a vehicle in the slightly curved, convex mirror it may seem further away than it actually is. Although convex mirrors give a wider field of view than flat mirrors, the image is slightly distorted. This is why you should always use your interior and

Convex glass

Flat glass

door mirrors in conjunction with one another in order to get a true picture of the road behind.

What you can't see in your mirrors

What you can't see in your mirrors is often just as important as what you can see. There are some areas behind that are not visible in your mirrors; these areas are called 'blind spots'. To compensate for this, in some situations you will need to look around over your shoulder in addition to checking your mirrors.

THESE GREY AREAS ARE NOT VISIBLE IN THE MIRRORS

When to use your mirrors

Mirrors should always be used well before you:

- move off
- give a signal
- change your direction
- slow down or stop
- overtake
- open your car door

Remember!
Mirrors
Signal
Manoeuvre

? Driving quiz
Rear view mirrors

1 The following routine is essential for safe driving:

MIRRORS – SIGNAL – MANOEUVRE

TRUE ◯   FALSE ◯

2 Do vehicles following behind appear to be closer or further away when viewed in convex mirrors as opposed to flat mirrors (tick one answer):

☐ **nearer?**

☐ **further away?**

3 There are six specific situations in which you must always use your mirrors and four of them are listed below. Fill in the two missing 'mirror' situations.

- **moving off**
- ? .... ⇐ ⇐ ⇐
- **changing direction**
- ? .... ⇐ ⇐ ⇐
- **overtaking**
- **opening your car door**

Progress check ✓

I can explain the limitations of mirrors and also how and when they should be used.

◯ Signed .... Date ....

I have demonstrated my ability to use my rear view mirrors correctly.

◯ Signed .... Date ....

Moving off
Practical lesson

The 'prepare, observe, move' routine

This routine provides an easy way to remember the steps needed to safely move away from the side of the road.

Prepare

Before starting the engine you must ensure that the handbrake is on and that the gear lever is in the neutral position.

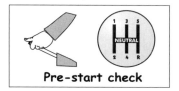

Pre-start check

> **Clutch down, select first gear.**
> **Press the gas pedal gently and hold it still ('set the gas').**

Bring the clutch pedal up to 'biting point' (this is the point at which the engine sound changes) and keep both feet still. The car is now ready to move off but you must first make sure that the road is clear and it is safe to move.

Observe

> **Check your mirrors and blind spots.**
> **Take special care when signalling your intention to others.**

Take care with signal timing

Move

> **Release the handbrake.**
> **Bring the clutch up gently and when the car moves hold both feet still.**
> **Turn the steering wheel slightly and move out to the 'safety line'.**
> **Gently increase the pressure on the gas pedal and bring the clutch up fully.**

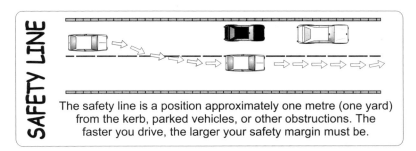

The safety line is a position approximately one metre (one yard) from the kerb, parked vehicles, or other obstructions. The faster you drive, the larger your safety margin must be.

? Driving quiz
Moving off

1 Complete the following sentence to define the two checks that you should make before turning the key to start the engine:

Before I start the engine I always check that the h...............................
is on and that the g............ l................. is in the neutral position.

2 You should *always* check your rear view mirrors before giving a signal to move off.

TRUE ☐   FALSE ☐

3 Draw a continuous line on the diagram below to show the safety line that car A should follow.

Progress check ✓

I can move off safely and under full control with help from my instructor.   ◯ Signed .... Date ....

I can move off safely and under full control without help from my instructor.   ◯ Signed .... Date ....

Lights and instruments
Training notes

Dashboard lights

On your instrument panel there is a range of warning lights. These lights vary from car to car and some cars have more than others. Some of the lights come on as soon as the ignition key is turned to the second position (your instructor will tell you more about this). The lights shown on this page are the most common.

Ignition light: This red light shows that the ignition circuit has been activated. When this light is on all the electrical accessories will work. If this light comes on when the engine is running normally, it indicates that there is an electrical problem.

Oil warning light: If this red light comes on when the engine is running normally, it is a warning of low oil pressure. If you ever get this warning you should stop as soon as possible, or risk severe damage to your engine.

Indicator lights: Some cars have two green indicator warning lights, one each for left and right; others simply have one light to let you know that you are indicating.

Handbrake warning light: This red light shows that your handbrake is applied. If it lights up when you are driving, check that the handbrake is fully released.

Brake warning light: This red light shows a problem with the braking system. In some cars it may be safe to drive slowly to a garage with this light on. Consult your car handbook for advice. If in doubt, park the car and call a mechanic – you might be left with no brakes.

Seatbelt warning light: This red light comes on if you, or one of your passengers, is not wearing a seatbelt.

Full beam warning: This blue light shows when your headlights are on full beam.

Fog light indicators: These lights show when your fog lights are on, usually amber for rear fog lights and green for front fog lights.

Rear screen de-mister: This amber light shows if your rear de-mister is switched on.

Pre-heater light: This is found on diesel-engined cars. You should not start your engine until this light goes out.

Choke warning light: This light (usually amber) shows when the choke is activated.

Instruments

The instruments (or gauges) on your dashboard will give information essential for safe driving.

Speedometer: The speedometer shows how fast the car is travelling. It is usually calibrated in both miles per hour (MPH) and kilometres per hour (KPH). The speedometer also incorporates an milometer (odometer) for logging the total number of miles that the car has covered in its lifetime. Some speedometers also have a 'trip counter' for measuring the length of individual journeys.

Rev-counter: This looks like the speedometer, but instead of showing the speed of the car, it shows the speed of the engine. Rev-counters are normally found in sporty or upmarket cars. The rev-counter helps the driver monitor how hard the engine is working and ensures that there is no engine damage caused by over-revving (making the engine spin too fast). The rev-counter is calibrated in single units, each one representing 1,000 engine revolutions per minute.

Temperature gauge: This shows the engine temperature. Engines are designed to operate at maximum efficiency within a set temperature range. If your engine is too hot or too cold, damage may occur and fuel consumption will increase.

Oil pressure gauge: This has a similar function to the oil light. However, it gives more information, showing a reading for the oil pressure at all times.

Battery charging gauge: This shows how much charge is going to the battery at any given time.

Turbo gauge: In cars with turbo-chargers this gauge shows the amount of turbo 'boost'.

Fuel gauge: The purpose of this gauge should be fairly obvious – it shows how much fuel you have in your tank. You should never let your tank get too low; this can lead to sediment, from the bottom of the tank, causing your engine to run unevenly.

Using the forward gears
Practical lesson

Why we need gears

Gears are fitted to motor cars so that the driver can use the engine as efficiently as possible. The gears allow the car to be easily controlled in a range of situations, at a range of speeds. The basic rule: change up through the gears as the speed increases, down through the gears when you need more power from the engine and there is not enough power in your current gear.

When do I change gear?

Gear changes are generally made when the car changes its speed range. Each gear has a range of speeds for which it is best suited; when you need to move outside this range, by either driving faster or slower, you change gear.

It is not necessary to change through the gears in any specific order; you can, for example, change directly from fourth to second gear. It is, however, very important to ensure that your speed will match the gear that you select.

Experienced drivers develop a 'feel' for when to change gear. You will quickly learn to develop this feel (with your instructor's guidance) by listening to the sound of the engine, feeling the vibration of the car or watching a rev-counter.

Making gear changes

The sequence for changing gear is quite easy and will soon become habitual.

Changing up	clutch down
	release the gas pedal
	move the gear lever
	clutch up gently
	press the gas pedal gently
Changing down	reduce speed by decelerating or braking
	stay off the gas pedal, and press the clutch down
	move the gear lever
	clutch up gently
	press the gas pedal gently

? Driving quiz
Using the forward gears

1 Number each of the steps shown below to demonstrate how you would change up from second to third gear.

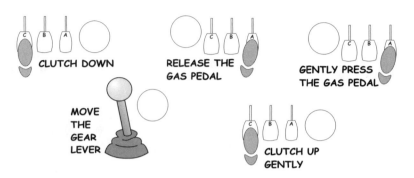

2 It is good driving practice to sometimes miss out a gear when making a gear change, for example, by changing direct from fourth to second gear.

TRUE ☐   FALSE ☐

3 Mark this diagram to show the position of first, second, third, fourth and fifth gears.

Note: Some cars have only four forward gears and in others – usually high performance sports cars – the positions of the gears may vary slightly

Progress check

I can change through all the forward gears with help from my instructor.

◯ Signed .... Date ....

I can change through all the forward gears without help from my instructor.

◯ Signed .... Date ....

26

Stopping the car safely
Practical lesson

How to stop

Just as there is a routine for moving off and changing gear, there is also a routine for stopping.

The routine is as follows:

- check your mirrors

- consider the need for a signal and give one if necessary

- foot off the gas

- brake gently

- look well ahead – not down at the kerb

- press the clutch pedal down just before the car stops

- pull on the handbrake **after** the car has stopped

- select neutral **before** releasing the clutch and footbrake

- relax!

Where to stop

The diagram opposite shows some of the places where you should avoid stopping. Whenever you stop, consider if you may be causing inconvenience to others and, of course, make absolutely sure that you are parked legally.

You can find out more about waiting and parking by reading the section entitled 'Waiting and parking' in *The Highway Code*.

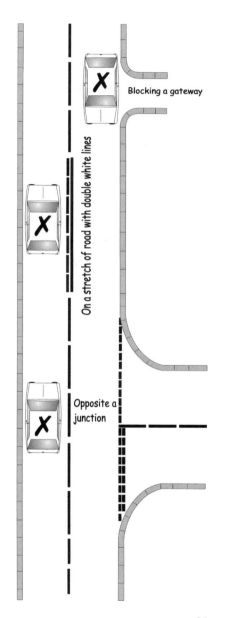

Blocking a gateway

On a stretch of road with double white lines

Opposite a junction

❓ Driving quiz
Stopping the car safely

Number the boxes on the diagram below to show the order in which each action is carried out when stopping. Box number 1 has already been completed for you.

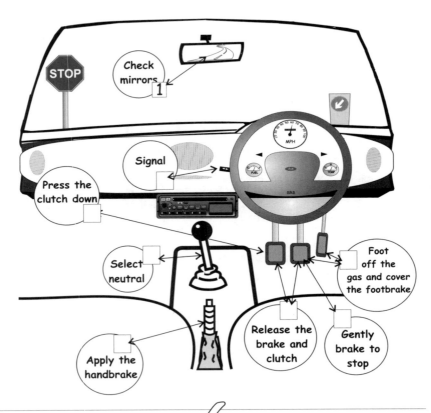

Progress check ✓

I can choose a safe parking place and stop safely with help from my instructor.

⬤ Signed .... Date .....

I can choose a safe parking place and stop safely without help from my instructor.

⬤ Signed .... Date ...

Steering
Practical lesson

Getting around things

When you have mastered the basics of moving off and initial clutch control you need to be able to steer the car. In order to steer the car effectively it will help if you understand the importance of the link between observation and steering.

In order to steer effectively, your eyes need to send the correct information to your brain so that it can send the appropriate commands to your arms and hands. Bearing this in mind, **the first rule of steering is: look at what you want to hit!** This isn't as silly as it sounds. What it means is: if you want to hit the gaps between obstructions you look at the gaps.

As a pedestrian you will be used to looking about five metres (five yards) ahead. This is fine when walking around at two or three miles per hour. However,

> This hand pulls
> This hand slides
> This hand slides
> This hand pushes
> This hand pulls
> This hand slides
>
> The pull-push steering method is generally accepted as the best way to maintain steering control in normal driving.

when driving a car you are going much faster than this. At 30 mph (walking speed x 15) you will need to look much further ahead. **The second rule of steering is: look well ahead.**

Because there are things happening all round when you are driving (and the scene can change quickly) you need to keep your eyes moving. This is similar to watching a film from the front row of a wide screen cinema. If you don't move your eyes you won't get the big picture. **So the third rule is: keep your eyes moving.**

If you apply the steering rules above you will always follow a safety line (the imaginary line plotting the path of your vehicle ahead). Finally, you must decide where the car is going well before you get there!

Look well ahead to follow an imaginary safety line that will keep you at least one metre (one yard) from the kerb or any obstructions

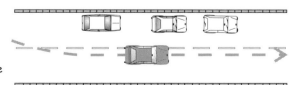

? Driving quiz
Steering

1 When steering you should concentrate on parked cars to avoid hitting them.

TRUE ☐   FALSE ☐

2 In order to steer correctly you need to scan the road, looking all around and into the distance. As a minimum, how far should you look into the distance when travelling at 30 mph (tick one answer):

☐ 30 metres (100 feet)?

☐ 50 metres (165 feet)?

☐ 75 metres (245 feet)?

3 What is the safety line (tick one answer):

○ a white line used to separate traffic?

○ the stopping place at traffic lights?

○ an imaginary line projected ahead for safe steering?

○ the rope used to secure loads on your roof rack?

Progress check ✓

I can steer the car safely with help from my instructor.

○ Signed .... Date ....

I can steer the car safely without help from my instructor.

○ Signed .... Date ....

Looking after your car
Better driving tips

Don't break down!

A breakdown, at best, is an inconvenience, at worst it can leave you stranded in the middle of nowhere, make you late for an appointment, etcetera. In short, breakdowns can leave you vulnerable and create all sorts of problems. The best way to avoid breakdowns is to plan not to break down. You can do this by carrying out a series of quick and easy vehicle checks and by having your car serviced at the regular intervals recommended by the manufacturer. A few minutes each week can greatly reduce the risk of a breakdown. The checks you should make are split into two areas – daily and weekly.

Daily vehicle checks

Every day you should make sure that the following items are clean:

- **windows**
- **mirrors**
- **lights**
- **rear red reflectors**
- **indicators**
- **number plates**

The alternative to good maintenance

Keeping these items clean will mean that you can see other drivers and other drivers can see you! (The law requires that your number plates must be clean and visible at all times.) You should also check the correct operation of the following:

- **headlights**
- **parking lights**
- **brake lights**
- **horn**
- **windscreen wipers**
- **windscreen washers**

What poor maintenance can do for you !!

It is illegal to drive the car with any of the items listed above inoperative.

Tyres: Make a quick visual check of the tyres each day and check the tyre pressures weekly. Walk around the car and look for any obvious tyre damage. Don't wait until your tyre bursts at 60 mph.

Weekly vehicle maintenance exercise

The best way to learn about vehicle checks listed on this page is to do them.
Carry out the following checks with help from a friend or relative, using their car, or
with your driving instructor. If you have a car of your own, use that. Look at the
car's handbook to find out about each check and then make the checks while
being supervised. The checks should be repeated every week.

Work through the list, and tick each item after you have checked it.

○ **Engine oil level** — Too much or too little oil can lead to engine damage that may be expensive to repair.

○ **Engine coolant level** — If there is a leak, or if the level is low, the car can overheat and break down – a common but easily avoidable problem.

○ **Brake and clutch fluid levels** — This sounds complicated but it is simply a matter of looking to see how full the relevant reservoir is. If these levels are low you should consult a mechanic.

○ **Screen-wash level and wiper blade condition** — If you check this weekly you should never run out. Dirty windscreens have led to several serious accidents – some fatal. They could have been avoided by this two-minute check.

○ **Battery electrolyte level** — These days most car batteries are maintenance free; if this is the case there are no checks to make. Most calls to breakdown companies are because of flat batteries. A well-maintained battery will last longer and will always start your car.

Tyres: You should also make a detailed inspection of your tyres once a week.
This involves checking the tyre pressure, looking for damage on the
inside edges (be careful of your hands when doing this in case there
is glass or other debris embedded in the tyre) and removing any
stones or other material from the tread of the tyre.

By performing your weekly vehicle checks, not only will you be safer
on the road, but you will also be keeping your running costs down. Badly kept
tyres wear out more quickly, neglected engines use more fuel and break down
more frequently. The checks only take a few minutes and can be done at the
same time that you wash your car or get fuel.

Skill development
Practical lesson

Practice makes perfect

You have now gained a range of basic skills. You need to practise these skills as much as possible before moving on. To help with this practice you will learn to use these skills in different ways with three new manoeuvres:

- uphill starts
- downhill starts
- angle starts

Uphill starts

Uphill starts are similar to level starts; however, you have to make the engine work a bit harder. You do this by using more gas. Because it will take more time to build up speed, you may need a bigger gap in the traffic than you have been used to before starting to move.

Downhill starts

When moving off downhill, gravity provides the power to get the car moving. To take advantage of this you need to press the footbrake **before** you release the handbrake; this will hold the car still. When you release the footbrake the car will start to roll, and you can then bring up the clutch and press the gas pedal (if necessary). If the hill is quite steep it may be appropriate to move off in second gear.

Moving off at an angle

Like the uphill start, this manoeuvre might be tested during your driving test. However, that isn't the main reason for learning it. When you have passed your test you will often have to move out from 'tight' situations. This excercise requires excellent clutch control, and you must ensure that you get all the practice needed to develop this skill.

When moving out at an angle you need to pay particular attention to traffic approaching from both the front and behind. From the front because you may swing into its path, from behind because you will be moving out slowly and other cars will catch up quickly. It is also a good idea to look around at least twice as you move to double check that there is enough room to move out safely.

? # Driving quiz
Skill development

1 When moving off uphill do you need (tick one answer):

☐ more gas than on a level road?

☐ less gas than on a level road?

☐ the same amount of gas as on a level road?

2 What do these warning signs mean (refer to *The Highway Code*)?

10% = ☐   20% = ☐

3 At least two of the statements made below about **downhill starts** are correct. Tick the correct statements.

○ The handbrake is released before the footbrake.

○ You must always use first gear.

○ You may sometimes use second gear.

○ It is not necessary to press the gas pedal before bringing the clutch up.

○ The footbrake is released before the handbrake.

Progress check ✓

I can move off uphill, downhill and from behind a parked vehicle with help from my instructor.   ○ Signed .... Date ....

I can move off uphill, downhill and from behind a parked vehicle without help from my instructor.   ○ Signed .... Date ....

Emergency stops
Practical lesson

Stopping quickly

Keep both hands firmly on the wheel

With the advice given in this book, and a safe and sensible attitude to other road users, you should rarely, if ever, have to make an emergency stop. However, we are all human. You may, at some time over the years to come, have a lapse of attention or meet another road user who suddenly does something that could not have been anticipated. In this situation you will need to be able to stop quickly and safely.

Controlling the car

Control when stopping quickly is easy if you follow the two basic rules below:

- keep both hands on the steering wheel until after the car has stopped;

- press the footbrake **before** the clutch.

Brake before clutch

Dealing with skids

Skids are caused by driving too fast for the conditions, accelerating too hard, steering roughly or braking excessively. Although skids are more likely in poor weather conditions, you must remember that **you are responsible** for your safety and the safety of others. Always drive to suit the road and weather conditions in order to avoid skids.

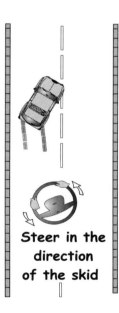

Emergency stop skids are caused by excessive braking. If you start to skid, take away the cause by quickly releasing, and then reapplying, the footbrake. By doing this, you will maintain some steering grip at the front wheels and possibly be able to avoid any danger or obstruction ahead.

If the car skids to the left or right, look well ahead and steer for safety. By looking where you want to go (as opposed to where the car is pointing) you will naturally turn the wheel in the direction of the skid; this in turn will straighten the car and help you to regain full control.

Steer in the direction of the skid

❓ Driving quiz
Emergency stops

1 Which of the following is the correct sequence of actions for stopping in an emergency (tick one answer):

☐ clutch before brake?
☐ brake before clutch?
☐ handbrake and footbrake together?

2 What do these signs mean?

A ....

B ....

C ....

D ....

3 Which way would you turn the steering wheel to correct this skid?

LEFT ○   RIGHT ○

4 What is the shortest stopping distance, on a dry road, for a car travelling at 30 mph?

☐ 12 metres (40 feet)   ☐ 23 metres (75 feet)   ☐ 53 metres (175 feet)

(You will find the answers for questions 2 and 4 in *The Highway Code*)

Progress check ✓

I can stop safely in a simulated emergency with help from my instructor.   ○ Signed .... Date ....

I can stop safely in a simulated emergency without help from my instructor.   ○ Signed .... Date ....

All-weather driving
Better driving tips

Bright sunlight

Although sunshine is normally welcome it can cause severe problems for drivers when it reflects off snow or wet roads. Bright sunlight can reduce visibility as much as thick fog when it shines onto a dirty windscreen.

Be especially careful when driving into morning and evening sun in the spring and autumn. Keep your speed down and be prepared to stop if you can't see the road ahead. Take extra care when entering tunnels or tree-shaded areas on bright summer days. Sunglasses provide the best solution to prevent sunshine dazzle. You can choose from polarised lenses which reduce reflected glare (good for winter sun and bright wet roads), photochromic lenses that get darker as the light gets brighter, or simple tinted lenses.

F-O-G – Foot Off the Gas

Fog is caused by droplets of moisture in the air. At its worst you can barely see the bonnet of your car. In these conditions it would be extremely unwise to drive.

Always use dipped headlights (or front fog lights) and high-intensity rear lights when visibility is seriously reduced. You must remember, however, that rear fog lights should not be used simply because it is dark, raining, or misty. Never follow close to the tail lights of another vehicle as this would reduce your available stopping distance in an emergency.

Holding your foot on the brake pedal at junctions will keep the brake lights on; this will help drivers approaching from behind to see you sooner. Open your window at junctions to listen for other traffic, then use your horn and listen for a reply before emerging. Keep your windows and lights clean and use your windscreen wipers and washers often.

Wind

The wind can cause severe problems for road users. Be especially careful when passing gaps on sheltered roads. A gap in the shelter that is offered by walls or hedges can affect cyclists, who may be blown into your path, and people, especially the elderly, who may lose their balance. Gaps in hills or rows of buildings can affect lorries and vehicles with trailers (for example, caravans). Cars travelling at speed can also be unstable in high wind.

CAUTION
Large vehicles can be blown off course in strong winds

LONG VEHICLE

Rain

Rain affects three things:
- what you can see
- what you can hear
- your grip on the road

What you can see: In wet weather your windows are more likely to mist up; avoid this by using the heater fan to keep air circulating. Windscreen wipers can become overloaded in heavy rain, but leave smears on the screen in light rain; get to know the different windscreen wash and wipe settings for your car to help deal with this. Other vehicles are harder to see in the rain; by using dipped headlights it will be easier for other drivers to see you.

What you can hear: Other vehicles will be harder to hear. This is because of the noise from the rain and from your heater fan; you can make extra visual checks through the side windows and door mirrors to help compensate for this.

Your grip on the road: There are no tyres available that will grip the road equally well in both wet and dry conditions. You can help your tyres (and yourself) by making sure that your tyres comply with the legal tread depth requirements. The tread allows water to be displaced and lessen the chance of aquaplaning, which occurs when a car is driven at speed through heavy surface water; the tyres skim the surface of the water (like a water ski), leaving the driver with little steering and braking control.

Beware! A light shower after a long dry spell in the summer can leave the road as slippery as ice. You will expect to come across ice in the winter – you are less likely to expect an ice-like surface in the summer!

Snow and ice

Perhaps this is the most obvious weather hazard of all. Despite this, many people have accidents in winter conditions every year. Get ready for winter by ensuring that both you and your car are fully prepared. Get your car ready by having it serviced at the start of the cold weather and by keeping a winter emergency kit in the boot (boots, warm clothes, shovel, torch, food, extra fuel can, etcetera).

The basic advice for driving in snow and ice is:

- don't drive at all if you can avoid it
- be fully prepared before setting out
- be gentle with all the controls
- use the highest gears when driving on snow
- slow down earlier than normal
- leave bigger safety gaps all around

Section Two

Road Procedure

Driver's Notes:

Giving signals
Practical lesson

Six ways to say hello

There are six legitimate ways to talk to other road users:

- direction indicators
- arm signals
- brake lights
- horn
- hazard lights
- flashing headlights

You should give signals if they will help or warn other road users. Your signals must not be misleading. For example, you might flash your headlights to say thank you to a driver who has just given way to you; another driver could see the signal and think that you are giving way to him. I'll leave you to work out the potential problems that might be caused by that misunderstanding.

Another common communication problem is caused by drivers who forget to cancel their signals after use. Although most indicators are self-cancelling, you should always check to make sure they are switched off after a manoeuvre. This is especially important after lane change manoeuvres, where the steering wheel may not turn enough to cancel the signal.

Changing direction?

Flashing indicators and the arm signals shown in *The Highway Code* are used to tell other people about changes in your road position or direction. This may seem obvious; however, many people forget that these signals are advance warnings.

If your direction signals are going to be useful to other road users, you must allow enough time for the meaning to be interpreted. As a general rule your indicators should flash at least four times before your brake lights come on. When using arm signals, make sure that you allow enough time for your other actions. You must have at least one hand on the steering wheel at all times.

Flashing headlights

Flashing headlights and the sounding of your horn have the same meaning: they warn other road users that you are there!

Ask your instructor for more examples of dangers that can arise if flashing headlamps are used for any purpose other than as a warning.

Many people think of the horn as an aggressive instrument; this is probably because it is often used too late. The horn isn't an alternative to the brake pedal. Use it early and always be prepared to slow down or to stop.

❓ Driving quiz
Giving signals

1 Correct timing of signals is essential for road safety. Mark the diagram below to show the point at which you think the driver of car A should give a left turn signal to turn into road B.

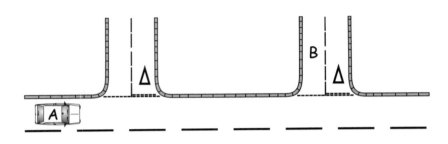

2 Complete the following words to indicate the six methods of signalling available to drivers.

D............................ I..

A............. S..................................

B........................... L........................

H................

H............................ L.................

F........................... H...............................

Progress check ✓

I can give signals correctly when prompted by my instructor.

◯ Signed .... Date ....

I can give signals correctly without prompting from my instructor.

◯ Signed .... Date ....

A hazard routine
Practical lesson

Using a hazard routine

A hazard routine is a basic drill, or system of actions, that you will use each time you approach a hazard. A hazard is anything that causes you to change your speed or direction, for example, junctions, parked cars, animals on the road, etcetera. By taking a routine approach, you will be sure that it is safe to carry out any action that may be necessary to deal with the hazard safely. The sequence of actions that make up the hazard routine is:

Mirrors, Signal, Position, Speed and Gear

The example below shows how you would use the basic routine to turn left.

Step 1: Mirrors

As soon as you are aware that there is a hazard ahead, you must check your mirrors to see what is happening behind. Just looking is not enough; you must ask yourself the question: 'Is it safe to carry out my intended turn?'

Step 2: Signal

When you are sure that it's safe to proceed, ask yourself if there are any other road users who need to know what you intend to do. If the answer is yes, give the appropriate signal.

Step 3: Position

Check your mirrors again to ensure that it's safe to move into the correct position for the manoeuvre (it's not necessary to change position for this left turn).

Steps 4 and 5: Speed and Gear

Use the footbrake to ensure that you have plenty of time to change gear **before** the hazard. If things seem rushed, you're going too fast. Make a final observation check all around and then complete your manoeuvre.

Observation

While carrying out the hazard routine you must keep a constant look-out for other road users so that you have all the information you need to make the correct decisions about your intended actions.

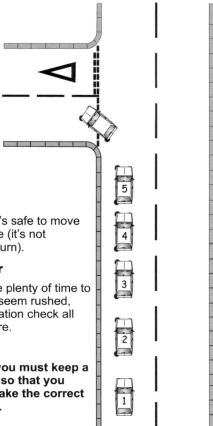

? Driving quiz
A hazard routine

1 Sort the following steps of the hazard routine into the correct order by numbering them 1 to 5.

○ **Signal**

○ **Gear**

○ **Speed**

○ **Mirrors**

○ **Position**

LOOK!
There are several suggested systems to approach hazards. Some say that you should look out for other road users at specific points. Our system suggests that you should be looking out for other road users and changing traffic conditions *all the time.*

2 From now on, the hazard routine will come into almost every aspect of your driving, so it is essential that you understand it fully. Think about the following questions. If you have any doubts about the answers ask your instructor to explain the routine to you again.

● **Why is it important to always check the mirrors before signalling?**

● **Can you think of any problems that could be caused if you started to change your road position before considering whether a signal was necessary or not?**

● **Are there any situations where slowing down before moving into the correct road position could cause frustration to other drivers?**

● **What might happen if you tried to change gear before you had adjusted your speed correctly?**

Progress check ✓

I can use a hazard routine to deal with simple hazards (parked cars, etcetera) with assistance where required.

○ Signed .... Date ....

Meeting other vehicles
Practical lesson

What is 'meeting'?

Every time another vehicle approaches you 'meet' and then 'pass'. However, the term 'meeting' is normally reserved for situations where the gap you are approaching isn't big enough for two vehicles to fit through safely and where one driver has to yield. This could be because the road narrows, there are road works, parked cars or other obstructions.

Who gives way?

Usually, if the obstruction is on your side of the road you will give way because you need to cross into the approaching driver's road space in order to carry on. However, sometimes the other driver may slow down or stop to give you priority so you must always stay alert to the developing situation ahead.

If the obstruction is on the other side of the road, you should have priority – **BUT** (a great big but!), **don't assume that the other driver will yield.** Always drive at a speed that will enable you to stop safely if the other driver comes through. If there are obstructions on both sides you must slow down and be prepared to give way. Usually the driver who arrives at the gap first will go through first but there are no hard and fast rules.

Using the hazard routine

As soon as you see an obstruction ahead (on either side), use your *mirrors*. You will need to change your speed and/or position and so must know how this action will affect drivers behind you before you can safely proceed. Next, consider a *signal*. You may need to give a signal to pass the obstruction; however, in most cases your road *position* will be enough to tell drivers behind that you are moving out. After checking your mirrors and signalling (if required) consider the position you need to adopt. Move out early if you are not stopping; don't get too close to the obstruction if you are stopping. Finally, adjust your *speed* and select the appropriate *gear* to match that speed. **If in doubt, you must stop until you have a clear idea of what to do.**

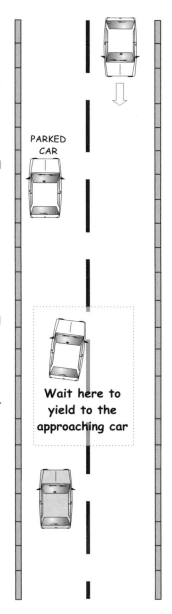

PARKED
CAR

Wait here to
yield to the
approaching car

? Driving quiz
Meeting other vehicles

The diagram on the right shows a car (A) waiting to give way to an approaching vehicle (B).

(a) do you think that car A is stopped in a good position

YES ◯   NO ◯

(b) give two reasons for your answer in the boxes below

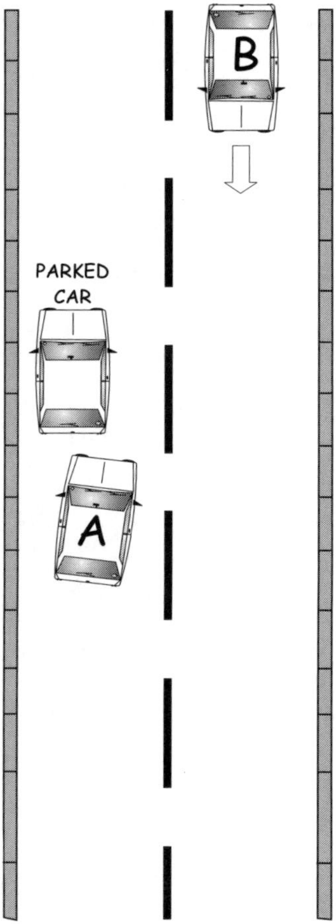

Reason 1:

Reason 2:

Discuss your answers to this question with your instructor or driving supervisor.

PARKED CAR

B

A

Progress check ✓

I can meet other traffic safely with help from my instructor.

◯ Signed .... Date ....

I can meet other traffic safely without help from my instructor.

◯ Signed .... Date ....

Straight line reversing
Practical lesson

Preparing for your driving test – and beyond

Every time you visit your local supermarket, take a trip to
town, or move in and out of a driveway or garage, you will
need to reverse. To make sure that you are ready for all
these driving situations, your driving test examiner will ask you to complete some
driving tasks which include reversing. The first step towards learning these special
manoeuvres is reversing in a straight line. This lesson will start to develop your
reversing skills so that you can tackle the slightly more complex exercises,
confident in the knowledge that you can drive backwards safely and correctly.

Some key points to remember

When doing any slow-speed manoeuvre, you will
need to watch out for other road users, maintain a
safe speed and make sure that the car goes
where you want it to go.

- observation
- control
- accuracy
- a neck like an owl!

Observation

You may remove your seatbelt to make looking around easier when reversing.

(A) and (D) Look out for pedestrians or vehicles emerging from driveways.

(B) Look to the front for vehicles that may be approaching.

(C) Look well back to steer a straight and accurate course.

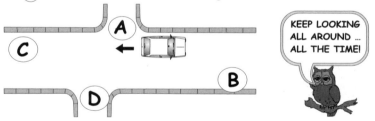

By the way, **owls** can swivel their heads all around. This enables them to take
Observation **W**ithout **L**imits. A useful skill for any manoeuvre!

Control

Use clutch control to maintain a 'slower than walking pace' speed
and hold the steering wheel with your right hand at '12 o'clock' .

Accuracy

Aim to keep approximately 45 centimetres (18 inches) from the kerb at all
times. Avoid touching the kerb as this can cause tyre damage.

? Driving quiz
Straight line reversing

1 What are the three main key points common to all slow-speed manoeuvres?

O...................................

C..............................

A..............................

2 Mark the diagram below to show the main areas for observation when reversing in a straight line.

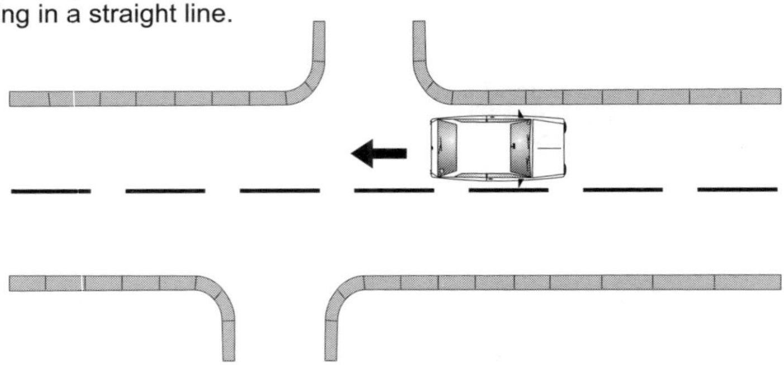

3 What quality does an owl have that you should try to copy when making any slow-speed driving manoeuvre?

What have I got?

Progress check ✓

I can reverse in a straight line safely and under full control with help from my instructor.

◯ Signed .... Date ....

I can reverse in a straight line safely and under full control without help from my instructor.

◯ Signed .... Date ....

Turning left
Practical lesson

Major to minor

This lesson covers left turns from main roads into side roads, gateways, or other entrances. It builds upon your current knowledge of the hazard routine.

You will have already made several left turns during your lessons. The aim of this lesson is to ensure that you gain the skill and knowledge required to take full responsibility and make left turns unassisted.

Making the turn

Start your hazard routine early as you approach the turn. When you check your mirrors, you must bear in mind how tight the turn is. The tighter the turn, the slower your speed will need to be. On very tight turns, give drivers behind extra time to react by signalling and reducing speed early.

Watch out for pedestrians. You must give way to anyone who is crossing the road you are turning into, or who is on a footpath that you intend to cross when turning into a garage or driveway.

Your signal should be given early, but it must not be misleading. Be careful with your signal timing if there is another road on the left before the one that you are intending to turn into.

For most left turns maintain your normal safety line driving position. However, if you are turning into a very tight road or gateway you may need to 'swing out'; take extra care in this situation, making sure that all other road users are fully aware of your intentions.

Second gear is the most usual for these left turns, so your speed must be 8 mph or less before you change down. If your view is restricted or the turn is extremely tight, you might need first gear.

Finally, make sure that it is safe to turn. Check your left door mirror for cyclists, look ahead for turning vehicles, look into the new road for parked cars or vehicles approaching on the wrong side of the road. After you have turned, make sure that your signal is cancelled and check your mirrors again.

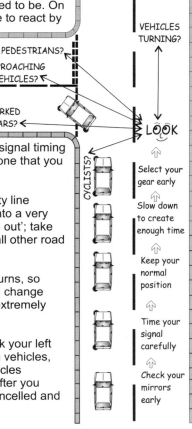

VEHICLES TURNING?

PEDESTRIANS?
APPROACHING VEHICLES?
PARKED CARS?
CYCLISTS?

LOOK

Select your gear early

Slow down to create enough time

Keep your normal position

Time your signal carefully

Check your mirrors early

❓ Driving quiz
Turning left

1 Mark the diagram below to show where you would look, and what you would look for, immediately before turning left.

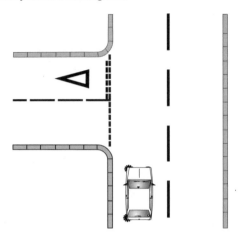

2 What do these road signs mean (refer to *The Highway Code* or your instructor)?

Progress check ✓

I can turn left from a major road into a minor road, using the full hazard routine, with help from my instructor.

⬭ Signed .... Date ....

I can turn left from a major road into a minor road, using the full hazard routine, without help from my instructor.

⬭ Signed .... Date ....

Reversing to the left
Practical lesson

Observation, control and accuracy

Remember these three key manoeuvring words from your straight line reverse exercise? This manoeuvre is simply a development of your **observation**, **control** and **accuracy** skills when reversing.

Good **observation** is essential for safe reversing to the left; you must be aware of what is happening all around you throughout the manoeuvre. As well as a general awareness, you must make some specific observation checks; these are shown on the diagram below.

Use **clutch control** to keep your speed to a slow walking pace. This will give you plenty of time for observation and steering adjustments.

Your position should be **accurate** to within about 45 centimetres (18 inches) from the kerb. In order to achieve this you might find it useful to use reference points to guide you in early practice. To do this simply line the kerb up with a suitable point in the rear or side window. Once you become proficient, you won't need the reference points.

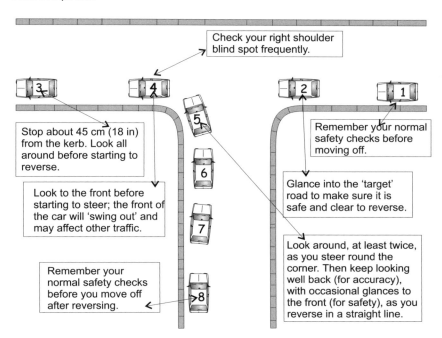

Check your right shoulder blind spot frequently.

Stop about 45 cm (18 in) from the kerb. Look all around before starting to reverse.

Look to the front before starting to steer; the front of the car will 'swing out' and may affect other traffic.

Remember your normal safety checks before you move off after reversing.

Remember your normal safety checks before moving off.

Glance into the 'target' road to make sure it is safe and clear to reverse.

Look around, at least twice, as you steer round the corner. Then keep looking well back (for accuracy), with occasional glances to the front (for safety), as you reverse in a straight line.

❓ Driving quiz
Reversing to the left

1 Label the diagram with the letters A, B, C, D and E to show the points at which you must make the specific observation checks listed below.

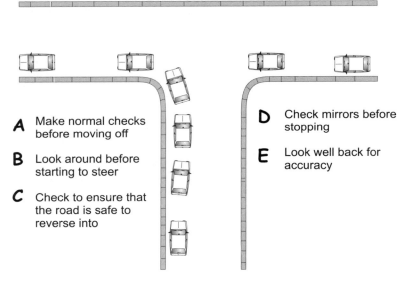

A Make normal checks before moving off

B Look around before starting to steer

C Check to ensure that the road is safe to reverse into

D Check mirrors before stopping

E Look well back for accuracy

2 When reversing around a corner you should be approximately:

◯ 10 centimetres (4 inches) from the kerb
◯ 30 centimetres (12 inches) from the kerb
◯ 45 centimetres (18 inches) from the kerb
◯ 90 centimetres (36 inches) from the kerb

Progress check

I can reverse around a corner to the left safely and correctly with help from my instructor.

◯ Signed .... Date ....

I can reverse around a corner to the left safely and correctly without help from my instructor.

◯ Signed .... Date ....

Emerging at T-junctions
Practical lesson

What is 'emerging'?

You 'emerge' every time that you leave one road to enter or cross another. Many busy T-junctions are marked with double broken **GIVE WAY** lines and/or signs (junction A below); these indicate that you must give priority to traffic on the major road; however, if the road is clear you may proceed without stopping. If the view (zone of vision) is severely restricted there will be a solid **STOP** line and/or sign (junction B below); when you arrive at the junction **you must stop**. You may also come across junctions with no markings at all. In these situations you must exercise extreme caution and always be prepared to give way to other traffic.

As you approach the junction, you must look out for signs or markings and use the hazard routine. Check your mirrors and signal as you normally would and then position for your turn. If you are turning left keep to your normal safety line (A). If you are turning right take up a position just left of the centre line and remain parallel to the line when you arrive at the junction (B). Start to look into the junction as you approach to assess the traffic conditions in the road that you are intending to enter.

Your speed will be determined by the type of junction and your zone of vision. If you are approaching a **GIVE WAY** sign or an unmarked junction, with a good, early, clear view, you may be able to keep moving slowly in second gear. If your zone of vision is restricted you will need to go very slowly and select first gear. When approaching a **STOP** sign you will normally slow down and stop without changing gear. Change to first gear after you have stopped.

When you arrive at the junction, look both ways for gaps in the traffic, in the same way as you would when crossing the road on foot. Drive on as soon as you can do so without causing inconvenience to other road users. (You must not force others to change direction, slow down or stop.)

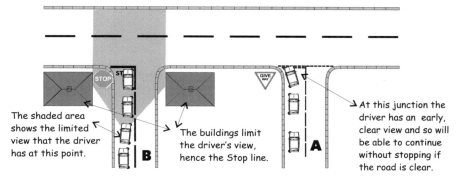

The shaded area shows the limited view that the driver has at this point.

B

The buildings limit the driver's view, hence the Stop line.

A

At this junction the driver has an early, clear view and so will be able to continue without stopping if the road is clear.

? Driving quiz
Emerging at T-junctions

1 Mark the diagram below to show:

   a how far forward car A must be before the driver can see clearly enough
      to make the decision to move off into the major road

   b the zone of vision of driver B

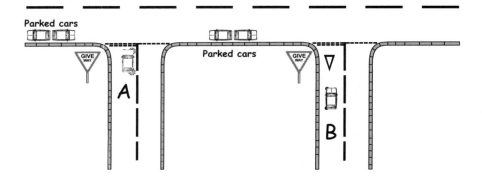

2 When you see the sign illustrated below, you must always stop.

TRUE ☐   FALSE ☐

Progress check ✓

I can approach, and turn left and right
safely at T-junctions with help from   ◯ Signed .... Date ....
my instructor.

I can approach, and turn left and right
safely at T-junctions without help from   ◯ Signed .... Date ....
my instructor.

Turning right
Practical lesson

Crossing the path of others

You should now be using the hazard routine every time you approach a junction to turn left. Right turns require the same approach sequence.

Check your **mirrors** early. Is there anyone overtaking? Is it safe to make the turn? When you are satisfied that it's safe to turn, give your **signal** and move to a **position** just left of the centre line.

Note: Although your normal position will be near to the centre line, you must make sure you leave enough room for approaching traffic to pass. You must take special care if there are cars parked on the right-hand side of the road.

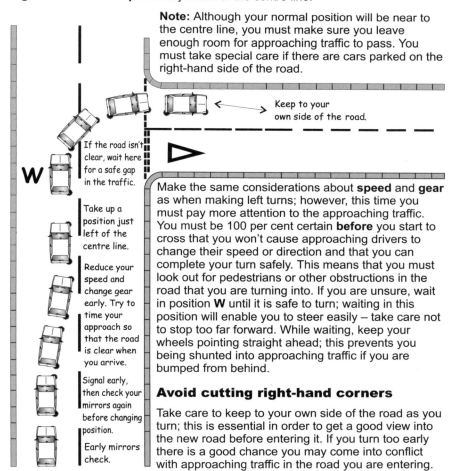

Keep to your own side of the road.

If the road isn't clear, wait here for a safe gap in the traffic.

W

Take up a position just left of the centre line.

Reduce your speed and change gear early. Try to time your approach so that the road is clear when you arrive.

Signal early, then check your mirrors again before changing position.

Early mirrors check.

Make the same considerations about **speed** and **gear** as when making left turns; however, this time you must pay more attention to the approaching traffic. You must be 100 per cent certain **before** you start to cross that you won't cause approaching drivers to change their speed or direction and that you can complete your turn safely. This means that you must look out for pedestrians or other obstructions in the road that you are turning into. If you are unsure, wait in position **W** until it is safe to turn; waiting in this position will enable you to steer easily – take care not to stop too far forward. While waiting, keep your wheels pointing straight ahead; this prevents you being shunted into approaching traffic if you are bumped from behind.

Avoid cutting right-hand corners

Take care to keep to your own side of the road as you turn; this is essential in order to get a good view into the new road before entering it. If you turn too early there is a good chance you may come into conflict with approaching traffic in the road you are entering.

? Driving quiz
Turning right

1 Mark the diagram below to show where you think you would wait if you had to stop to give way to car A, when turning right from road X into road Y.

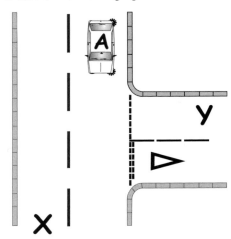

2 What do these road signs mean (refer to *The Highway Code* or your instructor)?

Progress check ✓

I can turn right and cross the path of other traffic safely with help from my instructor.

◯ Signed .... Date ....

I can turn right and cross the path of other traffic safely without help from my instructor.

◯ Signed .... Date ....

Turning the car around
Practical lesson

The turn-in-the-road

This manoeuvre is sometimes called the three-point turn but this term is a little misleading. The turn doesn't have to be completed in three movements. The number of moves required will depend upon the size and steering capabilities of your car, the width of the road and your driving skills. You will be required to do this manoeuvre as part of your driving test; however, this is not the main reason for including it here. After you have passed your test, you will need the same skills in car parks, garages, tight driveways, petrol stations, etcetera.

Using your current skills

The turn-in-the-road uses some of the driving skills you have already mastered:

- angle start
- clutch control
- uphill start
- observation skills
- reversing skills
- right turn skills

Camber

Roads are usually curved to allow rain to run into the gutter; this curve is called camber. An awareness of the camber helps control when turning the car around.

Observation, control and accuracy

While completing this manoeuvre you must be aware of the movement of other traffic, cyclists and pedestrians at all times, which means constant all-around **observation**. If other vehicles approach during the turn you should make eye-contact with the driver (your instructor will explain this in detail) and be prepared to give way. **Control**, as with all slow-speed manoeuvres, will be accomplished by careful clutch control. **Accuracy** can be achieved by brisk steering; keep the car moving slowly but turn the steering wheel quickly.

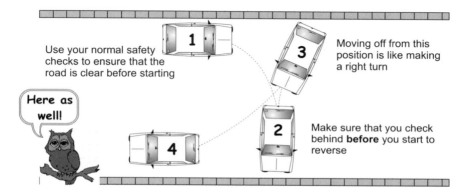

Use your normal safety checks to ensure that the road is clear before starting

Moving off from this position is like making a right turn

Here as well!

Make sure that you check behind **before** you start to reverse

57

? Driving quiz
Turning the car around

1 You must always complete the turn-in-the-road in three movements.

☐ TRUE   ☐ FALSE

2 Mark the diagram below (A, B, C and D) to show the points at which you would do the following:

A   the two points at which you would need your hill start skills
B   the points at which you should look to the right and left for other traffic
C   the points at which you will check your mirrors
D   the point at which you will look out your rear window

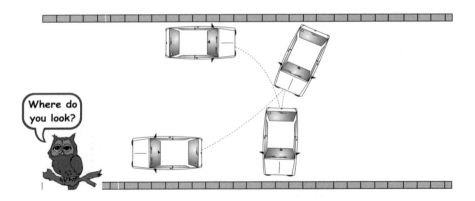

Where do you look?

Progress check ✓

I have all the skills needed to turn the car around in the road (listed on page 57).   ◯ Signed .... Date ....

I can turn the car around with help from my instructor.   ◯ Signed .... Date ....

I can turn the car around without any assistance.   ◯ Signed .... Date ....

Crossroads
Practical lesson

Dealing with crossroads

Crossroads are similar to other junctions you have done so far. However, there is an additional road to consider before making your decision about when, or if, to proceed.

By now you should be familiar with using the hazard routine approach, taking up the appropriate position for your intended direction. Because of the 'extra' road you will need to take special care with your observation, especially at crossroads with no markings. You must always approach at a speed from which you can stop safely if the need arises, **even when you have priority**. As you approach, keep checking to the left, right and ahead for other traffic, especially cycles and motorcycles (these are vulnerable because they are often difficult to see).

When turning right at a crossroads where there is an approaching car also wishing to turn right (see diagram) try to pass behind it (offside-to-offside); this will give you the best view of the road. **If there isn't enough room to pass behind, or if the other driver chooses not to, look out for other traffic that may be hidden from your view.** If in doubt, yield to the other car and wait until the road is clear before proceeding. Never try to beat another driver to the junction in order to go first – he/she might have the same idea.

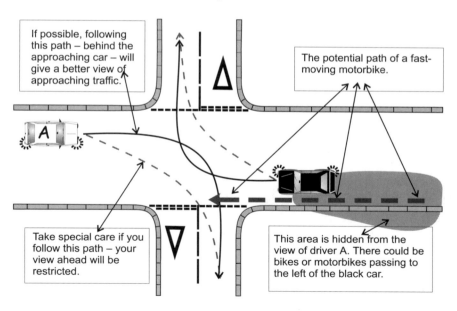

If possible, following this path – behind the approaching car – will give a better view of approaching traffic.

The potential path of a fast-moving motorbike.

Take special care if you follow this path – your view ahead will be restricted.

This area is hidden from the view of driver A. There could be bikes or motorbikes passing to the left of the black car.

1 Which group of road users are particularly vulnerable at crossroads, and why?

2 What does this sign mean:

   a location of crossroads?

   b crossroads ahead?

   c railway level crossing ahead?

A, B or C?

3 If an approaching driver wishes to turn right at a crossroads where you are turning right, you should try to pass offside-to-offside if possible.

⬜ TRUE   ⬜ FALSE

Progress check ✓

I can approach and deal with crossroads safely and correctly with help from my instructor.

◯ Signed .... Date ....

I can approach and deal with crossroads safely and correctly without help from my instructor.

◯ Signed .... Date ....

Roundabouts
Practical lesson

More traffic, less trouble!

As roads have become busier, the design of junctions has changed. In many places where there used to be crossroads there are now roundabouts. Roundabouts improve traffic flow by allowing streams of traffic to filter together.

Approach both large and mini-roundabouts using the now familiar hazard routine. Take several glances to the right to look for gaps in the traffic and try to time your arrival at the single broken **GIVE WAY** line to coincide with a gap; by doing this you will often be able to carry on without having to stop. The diagram below shows the rules for signalling and lane use at roundabouts. Read about roundabouts in *The Highway Code* to gain a more detailed understanding before tackling them in the car.

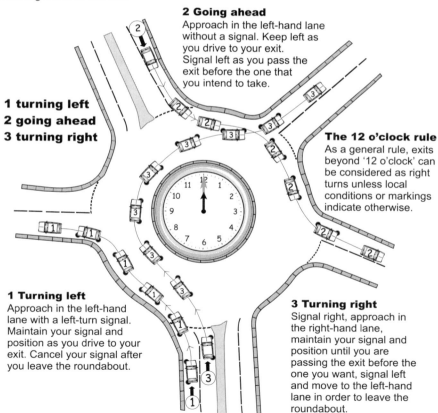

1 turning left
2 going ahead
3 turning right

2 Going ahead
Approach in the left-hand lane without a signal. Keep left as you drive to your exit. Signal left as you pass the exit before the one that you intend to take.

The 12 o'clock rule
As a general rule, exits beyond '12 o'clock' can be considered as right turns unless local conditions or markings indicate otherwise.

1 Turning left
Approach in the left-hand lane with a left-turn signal. Maintain your signal and position as you drive to your exit. Cancel your signal after you leave the roundabout.

3 Turning right
Signal right, approach in the right-hand lane, maintain your signal and position until you are passing the exit before the one you want, signal left and move to the left-hand lane in order to leave the roundabout.

❓ Driving quiz
Roundabouts

1 Label the diagram below with the path you would take, and the signals you would give, to enter the roundabout at road A and leave at road B.

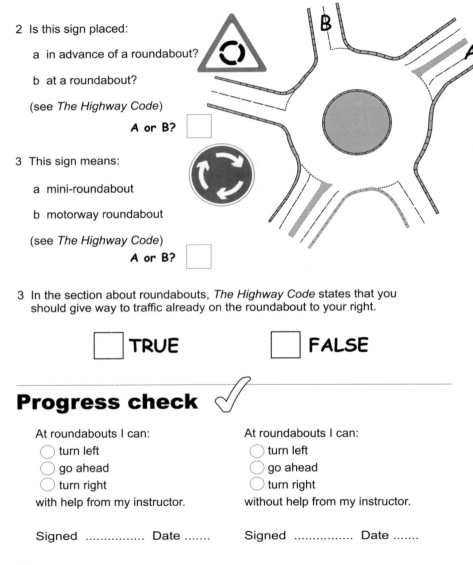

2 Is this sign placed:

  a in advance of a roundabout?

  b at a roundabout?

  (see *The Highway Code*)

        A or B? ☐

3 This sign means:

  a mini-roundabout

  b motorway roundabout

  (see *The Highway Code*)

        A or B? ☐

3 In the section about roundabouts, *The Highway Code* states that you should give way to traffic already on the roundabout to your right.

☐ TRUE   ☐ FALSE

Progress check ✓

At roundabouts I can:
- ◯ turn left
- ◯ go ahead
- ◯ turn right

with help from my instructor.

Signed .... Date ....

At roundabouts I can:
- ◯ turn left
- ◯ go ahead
- ◯ turn right

without help from my instructor.

Signed .... Date ....

62

Who's responsible?
Better driving tips

It wasn't my fault!

So often, after an accident, you hear people say, 'It wasn't my fault', 'The other car came from nowhere' or 'I didn't see him coming.' What people would say, if they were either more honest or better informed, would be 'I wasn't concentrating as much as I could have been', 'I wasn't fully aware of the situation' or 'I simply forgot to look to the left (right or wherever).'

All accidents are caused by the actions of drivers; it isn't enough to simply shrug your shoulders and blame someone else, even if they were primarily to blame. As a driver you have a responsibility to yourself, and others, to try to finish every journey in one piece. This means that you must use your powers of concentration, observation and anticipation to the full when behind the wheel.

Good **concentration** is essential for safety when driving. In order to concentrate fully you need to be relaxed. Is your seating position OK? Is the car too warm or too cold? Are you tired? Are you ill? You can control some of these things – your seating position, the temperature, etcetera – but what can you do if you are tired or ill? The best advice is: don't drive. If you must drive, make allowances by leaving greater safety margins.

Observation means more than simply keeping your eyes open. As you gain more experience you will recognise the importance of looking 'actively', that is, you will be on the look-out for signs, road markings, developing traffic situations, pedestrian movement and so forth all the time.

As your observation improves you will need to develop your **anticipation.** Good observation won't help you if you don't act sensibly upon what you see. Try to think of yourself as a 'driving detective'. Don't simply take things at face value.

A simple example of anticipation (or detective work) would be your reaction to road signs. For example, when you see the sign illustrated above, on a strange road, what do you expect? If you have a keen sense of anticipation you might expect any of the following: children on horses; dogs running free; perhaps a hunt with the possibility of animals running out into the road; a racecourse with horses crossing to the stables and other traffic turning on and off the road. By being prepared for any potential eventuality, you will be less likely to be taken by surprise. The driver without good **concentration, observation** and **anticipation** will not even see the sign, let alone consider the consequences.

? Driving quiz
Who's responsible?

Who do you think was responsible for the accident shown below? The driver of sports car A, who was signalling left, drove across the path of driver B, who was unable to stop in time.

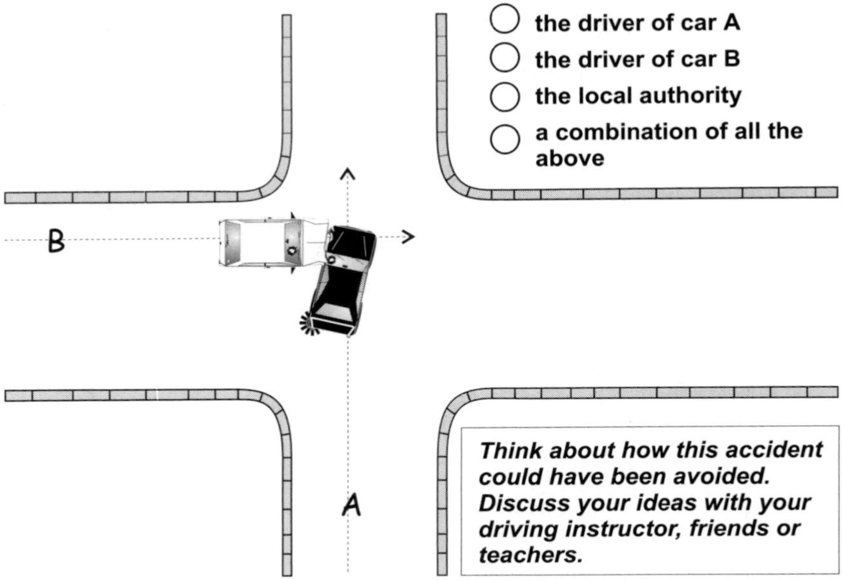

○ the driver of car A
○ the driver of car B
○ the local authority
○ a combination of all the above

B → →

A

Think about how this accident could have been avoided. Discuss your ideas with your driving instructor, friends or teachers.

Notes:

You are on the right lines if you don't know who is to blame. How could the accident have been avoided?

The safety bubble
Training notes

That certainly makes sense to me!

Space travel

Astronauts don't need the skill of controlling the 'space' around their rockets – there is virtually no chance of them bumping into another spaceship, nor of them being hit from behind! Drivers, on the other hand, need to keep a safe space between their vehicles and other road users, bollards, trees and walls, etcetera – the safety bubble.

The two-second rule

The safety space in front is the easiest one for you to control. You can adjust the gap between yourself and the vehicle in front by simply varying your speed. Your forward safety gap must always be large enough for you to stop safely if necessary; an easy way to maintain this gap on a dry road is to use the 'two-second rule'.

First, you must watch for the vehicle ahead to pass a fixed marker point. This can be a tree, a phone box, a lamp-post, a motorway bridge or any other fixed reference point. As the vehicle passes the fixed point, recite the following phrase at a normal speaking rate: 'Only a fool breaks the two-second rule' – this should take approximately two seconds to say. You should have finished the phrase as, or before, you reach the fixed reference point. If you pass the point before you finish speaking, you are too close to the vehicle in front; pull back and try again. **In poor weather conditions your gap should be at least double.**

2 SECONDS

Keeping a safety space to the rear

If the vehicle behind is following too closely, you need to increase your forward safety gap. Doing this will protect you and the driver behind in an emergency because there will be enough room for you both to stop safely. Another easy way to control this gap is to allow the vehicle behind you to overtake; this will make no difference to your journey time but it will reduce the risk of a rear end shunt.

Keeping a safety space to the sides

You need space to the sides to avoid pedestrians, cyclists, oncoming vehicles, horses and many other hazards. You can control this space by holding back from narrow gaps until you are 100 per cent certain that there is enough 'room for error'. Allow at least two metres' (two yards') clearance when passing cyclists.

Other people's space

Remember, other people need space around them in the same way that you need space around your vehicle. Be considerate, never be a space invader.

? Driving quiz
The safety bubble

1 How long should the gap be between car A and car B on a wet road?

☐ 1 second   ☐ 2 seconds   ☐ 4 seconds

2 What is the easiest way to deal with a car following too close behind you on an open road when there is no other traffic about (tick one answer):

○ speed up to get out of the way?

○ brake sharply to warn the driver off?

○ slow down and let the other driver overtake?

3 When passing cyclists you should leave at least two metres' (two yards') clearance.

☐ TRUE   ☐ FALSE

Progress check ✓

I can keep a safety bubble around my car with help from my instructor.

○ Signed .... Date ....

I can keep a safety bubble around my car without help from my instructor.

○ Signed .... Date ....

66

Section Three

Applying Your Skills

Driver's Notes:

Reversing to the right
Practical lesson

The odd one out ...

When doing this exercise, as with all your special manoeuvres, you will be the odd one out, which means that you must be fully aware of what is happening all around, all the time. Your owl-like observation is especially important on this exercise because you are starting on the 'wrong' side of the road.

Take special care when crossing to the right-hand side of the road (see diagram below). Others might think that you are turning right into the side road. When you start to reverse, check all around and then look back over your left shoulder. As you arrive at your turning point it will be easier to gauge your position if you look over your right shoulder (at the kerb). Finally, look back over your left shoulder as you reverse up the side road. By observing in this way and making frequent checks all around, you will be covering the key 'danger' areas as you reverse.

Reverse well back along the new road, about five car lengths. This will enable you to safely return to the left-hand side without interfering with traffic turning at the junction.

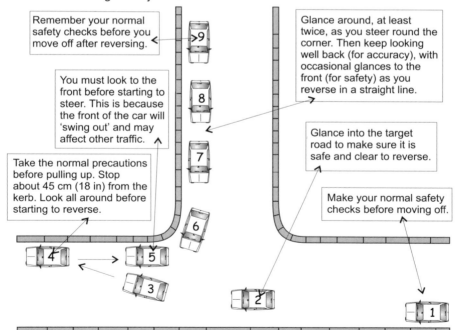

Remember your normal safety checks before you move off after reversing.

You must look to the front before starting to steer. This is because the front of the car will 'swing out' and may affect other traffic.

Take the normal precautions before pulling up. Stop about 45 cm (18 in) from the kerb. Look all around before starting to reverse.

Glance around, at least twice, as you steer round the corner. Then keep looking well back (for accuracy), with occasional glances to the front (for safety) as you reverse in a straight line.

Glance into the target road to make sure it is safe and clear to reverse.

Make your normal safety checks before moving off.

Driving quiz
Reversing to the right

1 Label the diagram with the letters A, B, C, D, and E to show the points at which you must make the specific observation checks listed below.

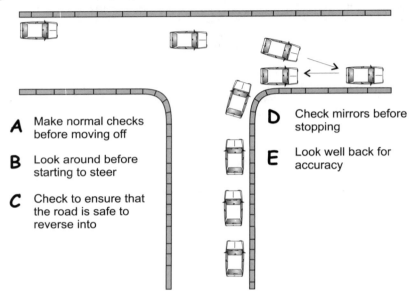

A Make normal checks before moving off

B Look around before starting to steer

C Check to ensure that the road is safe to reverse into

D Check mirrors before stopping

E Look well back for accuracy

2 If another vehicle approaches when you are reversing should you (tick one answer):

○ speed up to finish the manoeuvre quickly?
○ wave the other driver past?
○ ignore the other driver and carry on with your manoeuvre?
○ stop and see what the other driver is going to do?

Progress check

I can reverse around a corner to the right safely and correctly with help from my instructor. ○ Signed .... Date ....

I can reverse around a corner to the right safely and correctly without help from my instructor. ○ Signed .... Date ....

Reversing into a parking bay
Practical lesson

An everyday manoeuvre

These days, wherever you go, you will probably end up parking in a car park. In 1999 the option of testing your ability to do this was introduced into the driving test for the first time. As part of your test you might be asked to reverse into a parking bay at the test centre.

With a little practice you will soon become competent and confident at reversing into bays. The benefits of reversing in, as opposed to driving in, include the facts that it's usually easier, and it's much safer driving out forwards rather than reversing out. In the unlikely event of being threatened by someone with malicious intent in a car park, driving out forwards will offer a quicker and safer exit.

Two options

You can choose to reverse from a 90 degree angle into the parking space (A) or drive into a position from which you can reverse into the bay in a straight line, or at least as straight as the space available will allow (B).

Stay safe

Remember that car parks are used by pedestrians. Pedestrians can approach from any angle in a car park and might not be paying attention to the traffic. Keep a careful look out, all around, all the time, especially for small children who can be difficult to see when you are reversing. Finally, make sure that you park in the centre of the available space to leave yourself, and the drivers and passengers of the cars on either side, sufficient room to open the doors and get in and out easily.

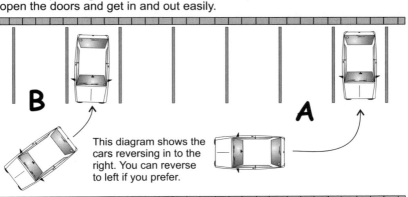

B

A

This diagram shows the cars reversing in to the right. You can reverse to left if you prefer.

? Driving quiz
Reversing into a parking bay

1 All pedestrians are vulnerable in car parks. Why do *you* think that it is especially important to look out for children? (Discuss your answer with your driving instructor.)

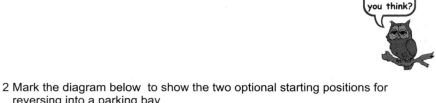

2 Mark the diagram below to show the two optional starting positions for reversing into a parking bay

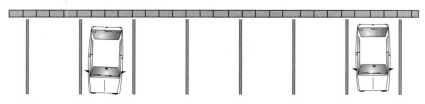

3 When asked to reverse into a bay during the driving test you can choose whether to reverse in from the left or the right.

☐ TRUE   ☐ FALSE

Progress check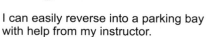

I can easily reverse into a parking bay with help from my instructor.   ◯ Signed .... Date ....

I can easily reverse into a parking bay without any assistance.   ◯ Signed .... Date ....

Reverse parking
Practical lesson

Save your legs!

Many drivers will walk miles rather than try to reverse into a parking space. This is because they were never taught this manoeuvre by their instructors. Learner drivers who have followed the *You've Passed* programme realise just how easy it is. You will soon be joining them!

Easy steps

1 Select a suitable parking position by looking well ahead.

2 Check your mirrors, signal if necessary and stop alongside, and parallel to, the car that you wish to park behind. You should be about a metre (a yard) away from it with the front of your car approximately level with that of the other car (position A). If for any reason it isn't safe to stop, drive around the block and come back to the space again.

3 Select reverse gear, and if the road is clear all around, drive slowly back, steering into the space. You should aim in at an angle of approximately 45° to the centre of the gap (position B); to do this you will possibly need full lock. As you move back, keep the speed down (a slow walking pace or less) and keep a look-out for traffic. If any traffic approaches, take the usual manoeuvring precautions.

4 When the front of your car is clear of the car you are parking behind, steer briskly to the right and continue to reverse slowly.

5 Stop, select first gear and drive slowly forward to straighten up (position C).

Be careful to ensure you don't hit the kerb with your tyres or rub them along the kerb edge. This could cause them to blow out at a later date, possibly when travelling at high speed.

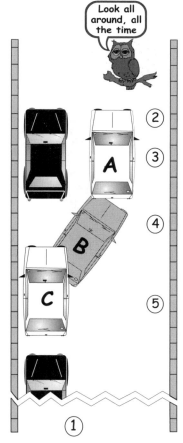

? Driving quiz
Reverse parking

1 Based upon your experience of other manoeuvres, what action will you take if another driver approaches while you are doing the reverse parking exercise?

☐ **Try to complete the manoeuvre as quickly as possible before the other driver draws level with your car.**

☐ **Pause to see what the other driver is going to do before completing the manoeuvre.**

☐ **Stop and wave the other driver past.**

☐ **Check to see if the road is clear and then wave the other driver past.**

2 Draw two rectangles on the diagram below to show the starting and finishing positions for the reverse parking exercise. In addition, label the diagram to show how far you should be from the parked car at the starting point.

Progress check ✓

I do the reverse parking exercise with help from my instructor.

◯ Signed .... Date ....

I do the reverse parking exercise without any assistance.

◯ Signed .... Date ....

Overtaking
Practical lesson

Do I really need to overtake?
Always ask this question before starting any overtaking manoeuvre. If there is a long queue of vehicles ahead, overtaking will probably not affect your journey time. If there is a dual carriageway ahead it will be better to wait until you get there before you overtake. If you are turning off soon it may not be worth overtaking.

Is it safe to overtake?
The obvious thing to look for is approaching traffic, but there are other considerations too. Is anyone overtaking you? Are there any turnings or gateways that other vehicles may pull out from? Is there a school or playground, etcetera? Make sure that you can see far enough ahead and that you can allow a safe margin for error if something unexpected happens.

Can I overtake on the left?
Overtake on the right except in the following situations:

- Passing a vehicle that has signalled to turn right and you can overtake safely on the left (you must not enter a bus lane during its period of operation).

- You are in a one-way street and can pass safely on the left. You should only do this when using the correct lane for your destination.

- There are two lanes of slow-moving traffic and the lane to your right is moving more slowly than your own lane (do not change lanes to overtake in this situation).

Let others overtake you
This doesn't mean that you must crawl around at a snail's pace letting everyone pass; it simply means that it is often safer to have someone in front, where you can see them, rather than behind. There are no gold stars for being stubborn and blocking the path of other drivers. In the worst imaginable situation you could end up involved in someone else's accident.

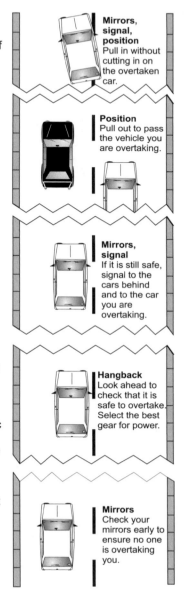

Mirrors, signal, position
Pull in without cutting in on the overtaken car.

Position
Pull out to pass the vehicle you are overtaking.

Mirrors, signal
If it is still safe, signal to the cars behind and to the car you are overtaking.

Hangback
Look ahead to check that it is safe to overtake. Select the best gear for power.

Mirrors
Check your mirrors early to ensure no one is overtaking you.

? Driving quiz
Overtaking

1 Name four places where you must not overtake (refer to *The Highway Code*).

2 What does this sign mean (refer to *The Highway Code*)?

3 *The Highway Code* states that if someone is trying to overtake you, if necessary you should slow down and allow them to pass.

( ) TRUE   ( ) FALSE

4 You can overtake on the left when (tick one answer):

- [ ] the driver ahead is driving too near the centre of the road
- [ ] the driver ahead has signalled an intention to turn right
- [ ] driving on a motorway

Progress check ✓

I know the rules and regulations about overtaking.	( ) Signed .... Date ....
I can overtake with help from my instructor.	( ) Signed .... Date ....
I have overtaken a vehicle safely and correctly without any assistance.	( ) Signed .... Date ....

Traffic lights
Practical lesson

Normal traffic light sequence

Traffic lights controlling junctions and road works follow the same sequence:

- RED
- RED AND AMBER
- GREEN
- AMBER
- RED

What the lights mean

Red: stop and wait at the stop line. **Red and amber:** Be prepared to move off. **Green:** move off if the way is clear and safe to do so. **Amber:** stop. You may only proceed at amber if you have crossed the stop line or are so close to it that stopping might cause an accident.

> Stop Line
>
> When the red light shows, you must stop at this line

Action at traffic lights

As you approach traffic lights try to anticipate what they are likely to do when you arrive. If they have been green for a long time, they might turn red. Use your hazard routine on approach, making sure that you select the best lane for your intended direction. Make sure you can stop safely if the amber light shows.

> This filter shows that drivers can turn left

Green filters

At some traffic light junctions you will see a green filter arrow. This means that if the road is clear and it is safe, you can move off in the direction of the arrow; you can do this even if there is a red light showing for other directions. If you accidentally select the wrong lane and a filter light shows, you should carry on and turn around later.

If the lights are out of order

If the traffic lights fail, approach the junction in the same way as you would an unmarked crossroads. Look out for traffic wardens or police who may be controlling the traffic.

Read about traffic lights and signals given by persons controlling traffic in *The Highway Code*.

? Driving quiz
Traffic lights

1 When a green light shows it means (tick one answer):

○ **go**
○ **go if the road is clear and safe**
○ **go slowly with extreme caution**

2 Base your answer for this question on your knowledge of traffic lights and your driving experience.

You wish to go straight ahead at the traffic lights (driving car A), but find that you have accidentally selected the wrong lane and are faced with a green filter arrow. Which of the following actions will you take:

a **carry on to the left and then turn around later in order to return to your intended direction?**

b **wait for the main green light to show and then drive on ahead?**

c **cross the stop line to wait in the clear space (C) in front of car B until the green light shows?**

a

b

c

Progress check ✓

I can safely negotiate traffic lights with help from my instructor.

○ Signed .... Date ....

I can safely negotiate traffic lights without any assistance.

○ Signed .... Date ....

Safety of pedestrians
Practical lesson

Three types of crossing

There are three types of pedestrian crossing:

- zebra
- traffic light controlled
- school warden or police controlled

Always be on the look-out for pedestrians, particularly where you see this sign

Zebra crossings

These crossings are marked by Belisha beacons – black and white poles with an amber flashing globe at the top. You must always be on the look-out for people near the crossing and be prepared to stop to allow them to cross. On the approach to, and after, the crossing there are zig-zag white lines painted on the road surface. You must not park or overtake within these lines.

Pedestrian traffic lights

The sequence of pedestrian traffic lights sometimes differs from regular traffic lights; at pelican crossings there is a flashing amber light. When the flashing amber light shows you may proceed if there are no pedestrians on the crossing. (Note: you must stop, as usual, at the steady amber light that shows before red.) Watch out for pedestrians near the crossing who may have pressed the button to activate the lights; use the hazard routine and be prepared to stop.

School crossing patrols

Watch out for flashing amber lights under a 'children crossing' sign; these indicate that there is a school crossing patrol ahead. The crossing may be manned by a school warden, traffic warden or by a police officer. You must stop when you are instructed to do so. Wait until all the children have crossed and the warden is back on the footpath before you move off.

As a general rule you should always be on the look-out for pedestrians who may step into your path. This is especially the case if the pedestrians are old, infirm, or young (under 15). See *The Highway Code* for more information about pedestrian safety.

? Driving quiz
Safety of pedestrians

1 You will find a Belisha beacon at a (tick one answer):

☐ **traffic light crossing**
☐ **railway crossing**
☐ **pelican crossing**
☐ **zebra crossing**

2 What do these signs mean (refer to *The Highway Code*)?

3 If the flashing amber light shows at a traffic-light-controlled crossing, you can drive on if the crossing is clear.

◯ TRUE   ◯ FALSE

Progress check ✓

I can deal with pedestrian crossings with help from my instructor.

◯ Signed .... Date ....

I can deal with pedestrian crossings without help from my instructor.

◯ Signed .... Date ....

Railway level crossings
Practical lesson

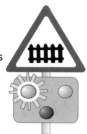

Something in common

There are several types of railway crossings including: crossings with barriers or gates; crossings without barriers or gates; and roads that cross one or several lines. All the crossings have one thing in common – great big trains! Trains often travel over crossings at high speed, which means that they must be treated with the greatest respect.

Look out for warning signs; these will give information about the type of crossing to expect. Use the hazard routine as you approach crossings and stop when the lights show. There may also be bells or sirens.

If you come across a half-barrier crossing – that is, a crossing where the barriers block off each side of the road separately – you must stay on your own side of the road. Never try to zig-zag around the barriers; the train will be very near. At this type of crossing the train triggers the lights and barriers approximately 30 seconds before its arrival. At crossings with gates, but no lights or attendant, look for signs giving instructions about procedure. You will need to be sure that the line is clear before opening the gates to cross. At crossings with no gates or barriers look for signs or lights. **When the lights are on, you must stop and wait, even if the line seems clear.**

Breakdowns on crossings

- Get your passengers out of the car and clear of the crossing straight away. Don't wait until the lights start to flash or the barriers come down; this may lead to panic.

- If there is a telephone at the side of the crossing, use it to contact the signalman. Tell him the problem and he will be able to alert approaching trains until the crossing is clear.

- If there is time, move the vehicle from the crossing. Try to push your car clear. If you are unable to do this, try to 'jerk' the car clear by selecting third gear, releasing the handbrake and turning the ignition key to activate the starter motor.

- After you have moved your car, phone the signalman again to inform him that the crossing is clear. If you are unable to move your car, use the phone to ask for further advice.

- **If the bells ring, or if you see a train approaching, you must leave your car and stand well clear of the crossing.**

❓ Driving quiz
Railway level crossings

1 The **first priority** in the event of a breakdown at a railway level crossing is to (tick one answer):

☐ move the car
☐ contact the signalman
☐ get your passengers out and clear of the crossing
☐ call a garage

2 What do these signs mean (refer to *The Highway Code*)?

3 What action would you take if you saw this sign (see *'Open crossings'* in *The Highway Code*)?

Progress check ✓

I can deal with (or explain the action to take at) railway crossings with help from my instructor.

◯ Signed .... Date ....

I can deal with/explain fully the correct action to take at railway crossings without help from my instructor.

◯ Signed .... Date ....

Dual carriageways
Practical lesson

Faster traffic

Dual carriageways often have higher speed limits than other roads. To accommodate this faster-moving traffic, dual carriageways have two lanes or more in each direction. Traffic moving in opposite directions is separated by a central reservation; this sometimes has a crash barrier to further protect the streams of traffic from one another.

70 m.p.h.

Although the average speed on dual carriageways is higher than on other roads (with the possible exception of motorways) there is still a range of hazards to deal with, such as cyclists, slow vehicles, traffic lights, crossroads, side turnings, gateways, etcetera. This means that you must exercise special care, especially when joining and leaving dual carriageways.

Joining dual carriageways

Although there are many conventional T-junctions and crossroads on dual carriageways, motorway-type slip roads are becoming more common. In turn these roads have acceleration and deceleration lanes. The acceleration lane is an extra lane on the left for use when building up your speed before merging with traffic on a dual carriageway so that you can join the flow safely. Deceleration lanes are found on exit slip roads; they allow you to slow down without holding up following traffic on the main carriageway. Usually, you shouldn't need to start braking until you enter the deceleration lane.

If you join a fast dual carriageway from a T-junction take extra care when judging the speed of traffic already on the main road. If you are turning right, wait until both sides are clear unless there is a large gap in the central reserve.

Clearways

Most dual carriageways are clearways (but not all clearways are dual carriageways). Clearways are roads on which you are not allowed to stop; stationary vehicles would pose extreme danger to fast-moving traffic.

No stopping

If you are unlucky enough to break down on a clearway, you should try to get your car off the main carriageway and on to the verge or into a lay-by for maximum safety.

? Driving quiz
Dual carriageways

1 Place a number in the circle below to show the speed limit.

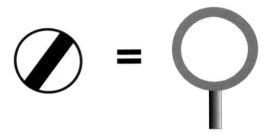

2 What would you use a deceleration lane for (tick one answer):

- ⭘ joining a dual carriageway or motorway?
- ⭘ leaving a dual carriageway or motorway?
- ⭘ overtaking slow-moving vehicles?

3 What do these signs mean (refer to *The Highway Code* or your instructor)?

Progress check ✓

I can drive safely on dual carriageways with help from my instructor.	⭘ Signed .... Date ....
I can drive safely on dual carriageways without help from my instructor.	⭘ Signed .... Date ....

Road markings
Practical lesson

More paint, more caution

Road markings are mostly painted white or yellow. White lines separate streams of traffic; yellow lines and markings prohibit waiting and parking. A general rule to follow is: 'more paint ... more need for caution'.

White lines

Roads in towns and city centres use the same system of white lines that are found elsewhere: lane lines, hazard lines, stop and give way lines, etcetera. However, in addition to these you will find bus and cycle lanes, and more hatched markings.

Bus lanes are provided to allow the free passage of public transport during peak traffic periods. They are marked by a broad solid white line and the words 'Bus Lane' painted on the road surface. You must not drive in a bus lane during its period of operation (indicated on the signs). You must also take special care when turning left across a bus lane. Some bus lanes can also be used by taxis and pedal cyclists.

Hatched markings are used to separate traffic streams and increase safety margins. As a general rule, you should avoid driving on the hatched areas edged with broken white lines. You must never cross a solid white line on to a hatched area.

Yellow markings

Yellow lines indicate parking restrictions. Hatched yellow boxes (box junctions) are used to help prevent traffic snarl-ups at junctions. The general rule is: do not enter the box unless your exit is clear. If your exit is clear, you may wait in the box for approaching traffic to pass when turning right.

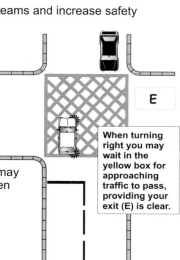

When turning right you may wait in the yellow box for approaching traffic to pass, providing your exit (E) is clear.

? Driving quiz
Road markings

1 Look at the diagram below. The driver of car A wishes to turn right. Can he/she enter and wait in the box?

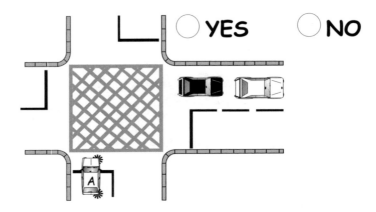 ⭘ YES   ⭘ NO

2 What do these signs mean (refer to *The Highway Code* or your instructor)?

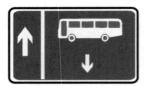

Progress check ✓

I can recognise and identify the road markings shown in *The Highway Code*.   ⭘ Signed .... Date ....

I can recognise and deal with a range of road markings without any assistance.   ⭘ Signed .... Date ....

One-way systems
Practical lesson

But I was only driving one way ...

One-way systems help to smooth the traffic flow around
busy central areas of towns and cities. For this to work well,
drivers need to choose the best road position for their
intended destination. Stay in the left-hand lane to leave the system via a road to
the left; keep right if you want to leave to the right. Always be on the look-out for
signs and markings showing the best lane for your destination and move into that
lane as soon as possible after entering the system.

You may occasionally come across a one-way system that has no road markings
(perhaps on a recently resurfaced road); in these circumstances you should use
your skill and experience to guide you to the best 'imaginary' lane position. In
other words, drive as if the lanes were marked.

Driving in the centre of your lane without straddling the white lines will help other
drivers recognise your intentions. If you are unsure about which lane to choose,
move to the right and drive around the one-way system again; this will give the
information needed for you to choose the best lane second time around. When
you are in the right-hand lane of a one-way system you must be particularly
careful to look out for pedestrians; they may step off the kerb looking in the wrong
direction and thinking that the road is clear.

Because vehicles might pass on either side in a one-way street, you must make
the fullest use of your mirrors. Be especially careful to make effective use of the
hazard routine whenever you change lanes.

Finally, try to get into the habit of filtering, that is, keeping the car moving when
you change lanes instead of stopping to wait for a gap in the traffic.
Ask your instructor to demonstrate the filtering manoeuvre to
show how it applies to your local one-way system. By keeping
your car moving, you will greatly reduce the risk of being hit
from behind by drivers who are not looking where they
are going.

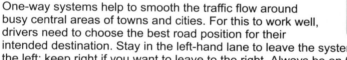

Keep moving at point A and
'filter' with the moving
traffic at point B

? Driving quiz
One-way systems

1 In one-way systems you should always drive in the left-hand lane.

◯ TRUE   ◯ FALSE

2 You should always be on the look-out for pedestrians who may step into your path; this is especially important when you are in a one-way street.
In which lane might drivers be particularly vulnerable to the problem of pedestrians stepping out (tick one answer):

☐ the left-hand lane?

☐ the centre lanes?

☐ the right-hand lane?

3 What do these signs mean (refer to *The Highway Code*)?

Progress check ✓

I can drive through one-way systems with help from my instructor.
◯ Signed .... Date ....

I can safely negotiate one-way systems without any help.
◯ Signed .... Date ....

Section Four

The Driving Test

Driver's Notes:

The driving test

Getting it right in theory

Before taking your practical driving test you must pass the theory test. While this book is not specifically designed for theory test preparation, by completing the quizzes you will have gained a lot of essential knowledge to help you pass. You will be exempt from the theory test if you already hold a full licence for a motorcycle or a car with automatic transmission.

The theory test comprises a series of multiple response questions and an 'on screen' hazard perception test. The best way to prepare for the theory test is to combine the learning of theory with practice. Your driving instructor will give help and advice on specific theory test preparation.

Getting it right in practice

When you have passed the theory test, you can make final preparations for your practical test. When it comes to practical driving tests, there will always be someone willing to give free advice about what will or won't happen on the day and what you should or shouldn't do. 'They never pass people on Wednesday morning'; 'Move your head a lot when you look in the mirror'; 'Mr Jones never passes young men on their first attempt'; 'The driving test centre in the next town is much easier'– **it's all rubbish!** You will pass or fail on your own merit. If you have listened to your instructor and are fully prepared for your test, you will find it easy.

The driving test was introduced in 1935, and since that time the single most common reason for test failure is probably the fact that people attempt the test before they are ready. Driving test examiners will confirm that as many as 25 per cent of all those taking the test are so ill-prepared that they wouldn't even pass with luck on a good day! At the time of writing, the overall pass rate for the test is 47 per cent. The latest changes to the test may lower the pass rate further and so it is more important than ever to ensure that you are fully prepared.

The driving test is designed to examine your ability to drive safely and apply the rules of the road. Passing the test does not mean that you are a good driver; but it does mean that a highly trained examiner considers that you are skilful enough behind the wheel to drive on your own without further assessment.

The best way to guarantee that you will pass your test early is to study this book and *The Highway Code* carefully and get plenty of practice and as much tuition from a qualified instructor (ADI) as possible.

Getting ready for the big day

Mock tests

You now possess all the knowledge and skill required to pass your driving test. The next step is to ensure you can use that knowledge and skill under driving test conditions. To accomplish this, ask your instructor to give you a mock test (or series of mock tests). The mock test should be as near as possible to the real thing, the same area and time of day. It should be completed without interruption, even if you feel very nervous; you can use the exercise to learn to cope with your nerves.

During your mock test your instructor, like the driving test examiner, wants to see your normal driving skills. Putting on a special performance would defeat the object of a test designed to ensure that your everyday driving standard is safe. You will be given clear and concise instructions to move off, turn left or right, stop, or perform one of the set manoeuvres. Although the main purpose of a mock test should be to help to prepare you for the real thing, and not to check if you are ready, you should be able to drive for about 45 minutes without making a serious error. A serious 'driver fault' is one that could lead to an accident, either in a different set of circumstances or if the examiner or other road user had not taken action to avoid the danger. If you can't drive without making serious errors, you will have little or no chance of passing the test. It's no use relying on good luck alone!

Applying for your driving test

You can get application forms for both the theory and practical driving tests from your local driving test centre or from your driving instructor. Tests can also be booked by phone or fax. Tests are generally done on weekdays between 8.30 am and 4.30 pm. However, in some areas it is possible to book a test for a Saturday or in the evening on weekdays.

If you are disabled, you can make special arrangements for a test of extended duration. In this instance, you will drive for the same length of time as other candidates; the longer appointment is provided for any additional administration or extra time needed to get into your vehicle, etcetera.

If you wish to cancel your test appointment after it has been booked you can do so without losing your fee as long as you give 10 working days' notice (excluding bank holidays and weekends).

Taking the driving test

The examiner

The examiner's job is to watch you drive and complete a report on your performance. Sometimes the examiner's supervisor will sit in the back of the car. Driving test examiners do not try to trick you or to catch you out; in fact, they will be as helpful as possible. Because of the nature of the job, examiners sit quietly and do not talk unnecessarily as this could be a distraction for you.

The test

The test starts in the waiting room. Make sure that you arrive on time, otherwise you might lose your test and the fee. The examiner will come out and ask you to sign a form; he/she will check your theory test certificate and photographic evidence of identity. Your provisional licence will also be checked to ensure that it is current and valid for the vehicle that you are being tested in.

You will then be asked to lead the way to your car. The examiner will note the make and registration number and will check that it complies with the regulations. He/she will then get into the car and briefly explain the test procedure to you. 'You should drive in your normal manner. Follow the road ahead unless road signs or markings indicate otherwise or unless I ask you to turn right or left.' This simply means that you should drive normally, as you have been taught, following all the relevant rules.

The examiner's language will be formal, but polite. For example: 'Take the first road on the left, please', 'I would like you to turn your car around in the road to face the opposite direction', 'I'm pleased to tell you that you have passed', et cetera. If you are unsure about any instruction, ask for it to be repeated. Don't, however, ask questions about how you should drive the car as this will meet with a polite 'Do what you would normally do' or something similar.

Your test will last for about 40 minutes and include a wide range of different roads and manoeuvres, including dual-carriageways where possible. At the end of the test the examiner will tell you the result and briefly discuss the test.

When you pass, you will be able to apply for a full licence. Whether you pass or fail you will be given a report form showing the mistakes that you made during the drive; this will help both you and your instructor to improve your future driving performance.

Typical questions about the driving test

Q. My dad says it's easy to pass the driving test. Has it changed over the years since he took it?

A. The test is more rigorous than it used to be. It lasts longer, the roads are busier, the marking is tougher and there's more extensive testing of manoeuvres. It takes longer to prepare for today's test but it is still easy to pass for those who are fully prepared.

Q. How long will the test last?

A. About 40 minutes.

Q. Which manoeuvres will I have to do?

A. You may be asked to do any of the following manoeuvres: reversing around a corner to the left or right; turning the car in the road; reverse (parallel) parking; moving off at an angle from behind a parked vehicle; and reversing into a parking bay. You may also be asked to perform an emergency stop.

Q What kind of roads will I drive on?

A. The routes are designed to ensure that you can drive safely in a wide range of conditions. Wherever possible, the routes will include: town centres, suburban roads, dual carriageways and rural roads.

Q. How are my mistakes marked?

A. The examiner will keep track of your drive on a form (Driving Test Report). The form lists a number of items that relate to your control of the car, its equipment and your procedure on the road. There are three categories of mistake that can be recorded. 1. Dangerous faults: these are marked if your actions actually cause danger. 2. Serious faults: these are faults that could be dangerous in a different set of circumstances or are habitual errors that are potentially dangerous. 3. Driving faults: these are less serious errors that detract from 'perfect drive'. A single dangerous or serious fault will lead to test failure. You are currently permitted a maximum of 15 less serious 'Driving faults' although it is planned to reduce this number to 12.

Q. What happens if I fail?

A. At the end of the test the examiner will explain the reasons for your result and give you a copy of his test report.

Q. What happens when I pass?

A. The examiner will offer advice about your driving and issue a pass certificate – you are now licensed to drive on your own!

Note: Rules for the test vary in Northern Ireland – ask your instructor for details.

Test day checklist

Tick off the items below to ensure that you and your car are fully prepared on the day of your test.

Your car

The car used for your driving test must:

( ) be taxed, insured and in a roadworthy condition

( ) display L plates to the front and rear (or D plates in Wales)

( ) have mirrors that enable the driver to see following traffic clearly while seated in the normal driving position

( ) have an additional rear-view mirror fitted for the driving test examiner

( ) The front passenger seat must have a functional seat belt and head restraint

( ) have all lights, indicators, brake lights, horn and other essential equipment (seatbelts, et cetera) in working order

( ) have clean and clear windows – 'L' plates should not be displayed in front or back window

Yourself

You must:

( ) wear spectacles or contact lenses if you normally need them for driving

I'm ready!

( ) have your provisional driving licence, your theory test pass certificate and photographic evidence of identity (see the test application form for full details of acceptable forms of identity)

( ) be in a fit and proper condition to drive

It is not appropriate to have a drink, even a small one, to calm your nerves. Remember – drinking alcohol and driving is extremely dangerous. Drinking and driving wrecks lives ...

Automatics, motorcycles and larger vehicles

It's automatic

If you pass your test in a vehicle with automatic or semi-automatic transmission, your full licence will be restricted to vehicles of that type. (Semi-automatics have a gear lever but no clutch.) The rules for driving an automatic are the same as for other vehicles and the test is conducted in the same way. If you want to drive a manual car after passing your test in an automatic, you will have to sit a further test in a car with manual transmission.

Being tested on two wheels

The general procedure for motorcycle road tests is similar to that for cars. Your machine must be roadworthy and you must comply with all regulations and provisional licence conditions. When you go for your test you must take along your CBT (compulsory basic training) certificate.

Typical gear lever for a car with automatic transmission

When taking the test your examiner will follow behind on another bike and you will keep in contact through a special radio headset (provided by the examiner). If your bike has no indicators or brake lights you will need to use arm signals During the test you will need to demonstrate complete control of your machine; this includes doing a U-turn and riding at slow speed. Remember that you are being tested to see how safe you are; follow all the general guidance in this book with regard to observation, positioning and response to other road users.

Large vehicle tests

Taking a test in a large vehicle requires all the skills outlined in this book. However, you will need to take specialist training to apply these skills in such a vehicle. Additional skills and knowledge required include the use of tachographs, rules relating to drivers' hours and rest periods, speed reduction systems (apart from normal brakes) and much more besides. The requirements for large passenger and goods vehicles are beyond the scope of this publication, but you can get full details from specialist trainers in your area.

Section Five

After You've Passed!

Driver's Notes:

Driving alone for the first time

WARNING NEW DRIVER!

Do you remember being told earlier in this book that after an accident many people can be heard to say, 'It wasn't my fault', 'The other car came from nowhere' or 'I didn't seen him coming'? This is especially the case in built-up areas, where the majority of accidents happen. Now that you have passed your test there is no one sitting next to you to help out if another driver fails to see you or if another car comes from nowhere. From now on you are on your own. But this is what you've been waiting for and working towards and if you continue to follow the advice given in this book and by your instructor you should stay safe behind the wheel.

For many drivers, their first solo drive will be in town. It's important not to be over-ambitious the first time you go out driving alone. Choose a route that keeps within a 15-minute walk from your home or destination; that way, if you feel uncomfortable you can park the car and walk. Don't drive for more than about 20 minutes, especially if there is busy traffic about. It's a good idea to choose a quiet time for your first drive alone – early on a Sunday morning is ideal. If you can't wait that long, at least try to avoid the rush hour.

Remember all you have learned about defensive driving. Earlier in this book there is an example of how you can be a driving detective (see page 63). Here is another similar example, only this time, the hazard is in town. A simple example of anticipation (or detective work) would be your reaction to road signs. For example, when you see a 'school' sign on a strange road, what do you expect? If you have a keen sense of anticipation you will first look at your watch. What time do children travel to and from school? You might also expect mothers with toddlers who are meeting children from school, so be careful passing parked cars. Is there a bus lane nearby – are there buses about? If so, there may be children crossing behind them. These are examples of the hazards you might expect near schools. Can you think of any more? By being prepared for any eventuality, you will be less likely to be taken by surprise. This is important advice for drivers anywhere, but especially in towns and city centres. Drivers who don't concentrate or who fail to maintain proper observation and anticipation will not even see the sign let alone consider the consequences. Remember, now that you have a solo detective's licence it's more important than ever that you keep looking for clues.

If you live in Northern Ireland, remember that you must display **R** plates for twelve months and keep to the 45 mph speed limit for new drivers.

Driving alone out of town

Stay on the road!

Out of town roads and country lanes have fewer junctions per mile than roads in town. This means there is less likelihood of conflict with other traffic. However, single-car accidents are more likely on these roads if you don't concentrate fully. This is due to higher speeds, road surface condition, sharper bends, mud and grit on the road and a whole host of other reasons.

The key to staying on the road is good observation and anticipation. This has been emphasised again and again in this book, simply because it is so important. The principle is the same in the countryside as in the town, but because you will probably be driving faster on country roads, you will need to look further ahead. The hazards you might encounter will be quite different as well. When did you last see a sheep in Oxford Street!

Drive defensively

When driving on rural roads you need to think carefully about every bit of information you receive. You will see several official road signs – bend ahead, cattle crossing, etcetera. The unofficial signs can give just as much information, sometimes more, and can help you with a defensive driving strategy.

The sign shown here is for bed and breakfast, but to a driving detective it means a lot more. A truly experienced driver will see this sign and consider the fact that there's a farm ahead, which means that there could be animals on the road, children playing, farm vehicles turning and so on. Care will be needed if overtaking near the farm in case something pulls out of the driveway. There may be mud on the road or (depending upon the time of year and the location) water spraying from an irrigation system. Last but not least, there may be a few newly qualified drivers! How do they drive?

Driving in the countryside, like driving in town, requires concentration and anticipation – it's just that the types of hazards you meet will be different. Thinking about the B&B sign, play the 'guess what's ahead' game to help maintain your concentration every time you drive in the countryside.

 # Driving alone on the motorway

Motorway safety

Many drivers think that motorways are more dangerous than other roads. This is not the case. Mile for mile, there are fewer accidents on motorways than on other roads. After all, many of the hazards found on ordinary roads do not exist on motorways. Generally there are no traffic lights, crossroads, T-junctions, parked cars, roundabouts, oncoming traffic, sharp bends, steep hills, pedestrians, cyclists, very slow-moving vehicles, or learner drivers!

Setting out

Before setting out on a motorway journey make sure that both you and your vehicle are well prepared. You must be alert and fit; if you feel tired, open the windows for some fresh air. If this doesn't help, leave the motorway at the next exit and take a short walk. Your vehicle must also be in good condition. Check your oil, water and tyre pressures, and make sure that all your windows and mirrors are clean. And of course – make sure that you have enough fuel!

Joining the motorway

You will usually join and leave motorways by acceleration and deceleration lanes. The acceleration lane allows you to match your speed to other traffic on the motorway before joining the flow. Deceleration lanes allow you to slow down without holding up other traffic. Always check your speedometer when leaving a motorway; 50 mph can feel like 30 mph after a long drive.

Driving along

Keep to the left-hand lane unless you are overtaking. If there is a queue of slow-moving traffic in the left-hand lane you can drive in the centre lane; this would be safer than darting in and out of small gaps, but you must return to the left lane as soon as the road is clear. When driving on three-lane motorways the outer lane is for overtaking only. Don't stay in this lane just because you are driving fast; you might tempt other drivers to overtake dangerously on the left-hand side. Things happen fast on motorways – stay alert to stay alive.

2 SECONDS

REMEMBER THE TWO-SECOND RULE

✓ Driving alone at night

DIP ...

Night versus day

Some people claim that driving at night is safer because it is easier to see approaching traffic. In some situations this may be correct. There are, however, a lot of things that you can't see at night. Your range of vision will be limited by the beam of your lights and/or the street lighting, which means that you will probably need to drive

Don't Dazzle!

more slowly at night, especially on country roads. Always drive at a speed from which you can stop safely if you see something in the beam of your headlights.

Getting the best view

Clean windows and mirrors are especially important at night when you have to glean as much information as possible from what little light is available. Make sure that your lights are also clean so you gain maximum benefit from them and other people can see you. Never wear dark glasses when driving at night; they might cut dazzle but will dangerously reduce your vision.

When leaving a brightly lit building to go to your car at night it takes your eyes a little while to adapt to the darkness; this can range from a few seconds to a minute or more. Give your eyes time to settle before you start to drive. Similarly, when you drive from a brightly lit area into pitch darkness your eyes need a moment to react – keep your speed down.

Dip, don't dazzle!

Switch on dipped headlights as soon as the light starts to fade at dusk. Drivers of dark-coloured cars need to use lights earlier than lighter-coloured cars. Use headlights on roads where there are no street lights.

When driving behind other vehicles at night, you shouldn't be able to see what colour they are; if you can, you are either following too closely or using full beam when your lights should be dipped. If the lights from the vehicle behind dazzle you, move your head slightly so that you are not in the direct line of the mirror. Most cars now have dipping mirrors to reduce glare from following traffic; these are operated by a simple flick switch on the mirror itself.

When you meet other traffic at night, dip your headlights. Do this as early as possible, even if the other driver doesn't dip. **Never** try to dazzle another driver deliberately, no matter how much you think it is deserved.

Problems

If you break down at night try to move your car off the road; use hazard lights and put out a warning triangle. Stay safe by parking carefully at night; if there are no street lights, leave your side lights switched on.

Driving alone –
at the scene of an accident

'There was such a mess ... I just didn't know what to do'

One day you could be the first, or the only, person to arrive at the scene of an accident. Or you might be involved in an accident but uninjured yourself. Would you know what to do? This advice is basic and simple, **but it can save lives.**

Warn others
Park your car with hazard lights or headlights on.

Reduce risks
Check the scene for danger, switch off engines, impose a no smoking ban.

Get help
Send someone for help or use your mobile phone (999 or 112).

Assess injuries
The quiet casualties are probably the most badly injured. Reassure the ` noisy ones that help is on the way.

Simple first aid

✓ **Don't move casualties** unless there is further danger (fire, chemical spillage, etcetera): you might cause further injury.

✓ **Check for breathing:** If the casualty is not breathing, clear the mouth (false teeth, chewing gum, sweets, loose teeth), very gently tilt the head back and, holding the nose, gently blow into the mouth at five-second intervals.

✓ **Stop any bleeding:** Firm pressure on a wound will stem bleeding. *Don't try to remove any item that has caused the bleeding.*

✓ **Don't give anything to eat or drink:** This can cause complications for medics and delay life-saving treatment.

✓ **Learn more**: Attend a local authority or a St John Ambulance first aid course.

If you have an accident

Read *The Highway Code* for information about your legal duties when involved in an accident. Finally, make sure that you are fully insured to drive your vehicle. Don't wait until it's too late to find out that your policy has lapsed. Apart from the heavy fine, you might have extensive claims for damages, claims that could run to millions of pounds.

Driving alone and avoiding accidents

Accidents are caused by people – not by 'other people'!

Rarely is a driver who is involved in an accident totally blameless. You should always be on your guard and alert to the actions of others. In this book you have already gained an appreciation of the potential dangers on the road. By taking heed of the advice and information given, the dangers will remain potential rather than becoming actual threats to life and limb.

Who crashes?

Common reasons for accidents include:

- excessive speed for the conditions
- failure to allow a sufficient safety space
- not understanding the needs of others
- drinking and driving
- drugs (prescribed and illegal) and driving
- tiredness at the wheel

By spending a little time considering the points above and how they might relate to you, you will increase your chances of living to a ripe old age.

Practical examples

By allowing a little more time for your journey or calling ahead to say that you will be late, you can avoid the excessive speed and risk-taking that kills so many people.

By leaving space around your vehicle and letting others overtake if they wish to, you will be more relaxed and safer at the wheel. For example, when driving on the M25 you might have 50,000 cars ahead of you and 50,000 cars behind at any one time; a couple of extra cars in front won't affect your journey very much.

Learn to understand the needs of other road users. Children often dash out without thinking, elderly pedestrians may be deaf or partially sighted and not hear or see you, elderly drivers might need more time to react, drivers of large vehicles need more time and space than car drivers, cyclists have wind and weather to cope with. Idiots should be avoided, not confronted. A good driver's list will keep growing …

Drinking alcohol slows down your reactions (think of slurred speech), and along with drugs and tiredness it warps perception. The only safe rule is don't drive after drinking, taking medication (or illegal drugs) or when you are tired. If you must drive, seek advice first (from a doctor or chemist) and take the utmost care.

Driving alone and avoiding road rage

The new menace?

Road rage is not new. It was first recognised in the USA in the 1980s. In the 1990s it became noticeable in the UK and is, unfortunately, now becoming more common.

Sooner or later you will be faced with drivers who cut in front of you, slow you up, overtake on the left, swear at you whether or not you have made a mistake, and who indulge in other anti-social behaviour. One definition of road rage is 'unchecked behaviour designed to cause harm to another road user'; often, however, the person commiting the road rage is acting totally out of character. Some drivers describe the 'red mist' which clouds their judgement. They get so angry they only concentrate on getting even with another driver. Sadly, drivers can all too easily be killed or injured when at the wheel in this state.

There are a few things that you might like to consider when thinking about road rage. The 'rager' is someone you don't know and are never likely to meet again (unless it's in court or in hospital). Their actions are not a personal attack on you but rather an inability to cope with their own emotions. As a driver it is not your job to enforce the rules or to teach other people a lesson. Many people are rude and thoughtless, and it's a comforting thought that they will only enter your life for a few seconds or minutes. They have to live with themselves for ever.

If you are ever in a situation where you are angry with another driver, take a deep breath and ask yourself this simple question: 'What do I really want?' When asking yourself the question, your expectation must be for something that is within your own control. For example, answering: 'I want to win the Lottery so that I don't have to drive to work' or 'I want the other guy to be a good driver instead of an idiot' will simply frustrate you further. How about: 'I want to be relaxed and safe'? When you have answered the question, 'What do I really want?', think about what you are doing to prevent yourself from getting it.

If you want to be relaxed you might have to ease off the power and let the other driver pull away; after all, do you really think he cares about your feelings and concerns? You might need to pull up, get out of the car and jump up and down swearing. If this is what it takes, do it. But make sure you do it on your own! You can control your feelings in the car in the same way that you control the rest of your life. Chill out!

Avoiding anger on the road needs self-control and patience. Road rage is often just as bad for the 'rager' as for the victim. On the next page there is a list of simple suggestions to help relieve stress when driving, which should help to ensure that you never 'lose it' behind the wheel.

✓ Driving alone and staying in control

Now that you have learned the basics of driving you can work hard to hone your skills over the rest of your driving life. Having read about road rage, you will be aware that there is a possibility that you may need other skills on the road above and beyond the ability to drive. Although the chances of a road rage attack are extremely remote, the following points will help you to cope with the stresses and strains that some people perceive to be present in modern driving. By choosing to adopt the appropriate behaviour and taking the correct actions, you will find that driving can be stress-free and enjoyable.

- Try to see the other driver's point of view. The car that has just 'cut you up' may well be driven by a fool who doesn't deserve a driving licence. However, it might just be that the driver is rushing to see a dying relative, or to witness the birth of his first child.

- If you make a mistake, hold a hand up to apologise; this often relieves tension for everyone concerned. After all, we all make mistakes.

- Avoid eye contact with other road users who seem to be challenging or aggressive.

- Leave room between your car and the vehicle in front so you can drive away from a dangerous situation if someone approaches with criminal intent.

- Keep your car doors locked, especially in towns. Keep your windows closed if someone approaches you on foot.

- If you think you're being followed, drive around the block or around a roundabout a couple of times. It might just be that another driver was taking the same route and hadn't even noticed you.

- If you know you are being followed, drive to a brightly lit place or a police station and make a lot of noise to draw attention to yourself. Try to get the number of the other vehicle.

If you follow the advice given in this book you will enjoy your motoring and the freedom and independence that it gives you. Above all, you will drive safely, courteously and positively.

As a final thought, try to imagine that the driver in front has been awake for 30 hours, the old man on the pavement is deaf, the cyclist is out for the first time on a new bike, the approaching vehicle has defective brakes and steering, the child on the footpath has a friend who is hiding and your front tyre is waiting to burst …